Social Networking Using a Tablet For All Ages

Jim G

BERNARD BABANI (publishing) LTD
The Grampians
Shepherds Bush Road
London W6 7NF
England

www.babanibooks.com

Please Note

Although every care has been taken with the production of this book to ensure that all information is correct at the time of writing and that any projects, designs, modifications and/or programs, etc., contained herewith, operate in a correct and safe manner and also that any components specified are normally available in Great Britain, the Publishers and Author do not accept responsibilit~~~~ (fault in design) of any proje~~~~ ~~~~ation of program to work correctly or to cause~~~~ ~~~~it may be connected to or used i~~~~ connection with, or in respect of any other damage or injury tha~~~~ may be so caused, nor do the Publishers accept responsibilit~~~~ ~~~~ failure to obtain specified components

Notice is also given that if equipment that is still under warranty is modified in any way or used or connected with home-built equipment then that warranty may be void.

© 2014 BERNARD BABANI (publishing) LTD

First Published – August 2014

British Library Cataloguing in Publication Data:

A catalogue record for this book is available from the British Library

ISBN 978-0-85934-750-1

Cover Design by Gregor Arthur

Printed and bound in Great Britain for Bernard Babani (publishing) Ltd

About this Book

Social networking websites like Facebook and Twitter allow people to exchange news and photos and make live video calls with friends and family all over the world. Research has shown that this can be very beneficial as well as enjoyable.

The latest small, light and very portable tablet computers mean that you can keep in touch with your contacts wherever you are. The material in this book applies to the hugely successful iPad and the top selling Android range of tablets, as well as tablets using versions of Microsoft Windows, the operating system installed on laptop and desktop computers everywhere.

Popular Android tablets include the Nexus 7 and 10, the Samsung Galaxy range, the Amazon Kindle Fire HDX, the Tesco Hudl and the Kobo Arc. As well as being a very capable eBook reader, the Kobo Arc, currently being promoted by WHSmith, is a fully fledged tablet, with Facebook and Twitter already installed.

Social networks require an uninterrupted Internet connection. This book explains, in simple steps, how to get online (and stay online) whether at home or while on your travels.

The book then describes downloading and installing 'apps', i.e. software, for Facebook and Twitter. Signing up and entering your personal details is also covered, enabling you to communicate with like-minded people to share news, photos and videos, etc.

The book also explains how to use the built-in privacy settings to control who can see the information you post on Facebook.

Twitter is another extremely popular social network, allowing short messages or 'tweets' to be posted on the Internet. Photos can also be included. As described in detail, you can follow the tweets of celebrities, etc., post your own tweets, join an online debate or promote a business, organisation or campaign, etc.

This book is written in simple language and avoids jargon. It will help the new user of a tablet computer to enjoy and benefit from using Facebook and Twitter with confidence and security.

About the Author

Jim Gatenby trained as a Chartered Mechanical Engineer and initially worked at Rolls-Royce Ltd using computers in the analysis of jet engine performance. He obtained a Master of Philosophy degree in Mathematical Education by research at Loughborough University of Technology and taught mathematics and computing in school for many years before becoming a full-time author. His most recent teaching posts included Head of Computer Studies and Information Technology Co-ordinator. The author has written over forty books in the field of educational computing, including many of the titles in the highly successful 'Older Generation' series from Bernard Babani (publishing) Ltd.

Trademarks

Microsoft Windows, Windows 8.1 and RT 8.1, Outlook.com and Hotmail are either trademarks or registered trademarks of Microsoft Corporation. Facebook is a registered trademark of Facebook, Inc. Twitter is a registered trademark of Twitter, Inc.

All other brand and product names used in this book are recognized as trademarks or registered trademarks of their respective companies.

Acknowledgements

As usual I would like to thank my wife Jill for her continued support during the preparation of this book. Also Michael Babani for making this project possible.

Contents

1

Introduction   1
What is Social Networking?   1
Uses of Social Networking   2
Requirements for Social Networking   3
    Privacy and Security   3
    Hardware Requirements   3
Tablet Computers — An Overview   4
IOS: The Apple iPad Operating System   5
Android: The Google Operating System   6
    The Standard Android OS   6
    Tweaked Versions of the Android OS   7
Windows: The Microsoft Operating System   8
    The Windows 8.1 and RT 8.1 Apps Screen   9
Social Networking on Different Platforms   10
    The Facebook Timeline   10

2

Getting Set Up   11
Connecting to the Internet   11
    Wi-Fi   11
    3G or 4G (3rd or 4th Generation) SIM Card   11
    Tethering   11
Wi-Fi   12
    Wi-Fi Away from Home   12
    BT Wi-Fi   12
    Using a Wi-Fi router   13
        iPad   13
        Android   13
        Windows 8.1 and RT 8.1   13
    Making the Connection   14
        Extra Notes for Windows 8.1 and RT 8.1   15

Checking Your Wi-Fi Connection   16
    iPad   16
    Android   16
    Windows 8.1 and RT 8.1   16
Restoring an Internet Connection   17
3G or 4G SIM Card   18
    Tablets with a Built-in SIM Card Slot   18
    Mobile Broadband Dongle   18
    Mobile Broadband Hotspot   18
Tethering   19
Key Points: Wi-Fi vs 3G/4G   20
    Wi-Fi   20
    3G/4G   20
Flight or Airplane Mode   20
Introducing the Web Browser   21
    The Web Page Approach   22
    The App Approach   22

3

Introducing Facebook   **23**
What is Facebook?   23
What Can You Do With Facebook?   24
Before Signing Up to Facebook   25
Your E-mail Address   25
    Security and Privacy   25
    Finding Friends   25
    Creating a New E-mail Address   26
    Signing Up   26
Installing the Facebook App   28
Signing Up For Facebook   29
Entering Your Profile Information   32
    Privacy — The Audience Selectors   32
Confirming Your Account   33
Launching Facebook   34
Facebook Features   35

4

Building Your Profile 37
Introduction 37
Entering and Editing Profile Information 40
Protecting Your Privacy 41
Uploading a Profile Picture 42
    Android and iPad 42
    Windows 8.1 and RT 8.1 Tablets 45
    All Tablets 45
Changing the Cover Picture 46

5

Finding Friends 47
Introduction 47
Finding Friends — iPad and Android 48
Suggestions 48
Search 49
Contacts 50
Browse 51
Finding Friends — Windows 8.1 and RT 8.1 52
Managing Friends 55
    Friend Lists 55
    Adding Friends to a List 55
    Edit Friend Lists — Android 56
    Edit Friend Lists — iPad and Windows 57

6

Using Facebook 59
Introduction 59
Signing In 59
Navigating Around Facebook 60
    The News Feed 60
    The Timeline 61

Posting a Status Update   62
    Posting an Update from the Timeline   62
    Posting an Update from the News Feed   62
    Writing a Post or Status Update   63
    The Audience Selector   64
    Posting   64
    Posting a Web Link in a Status Update   66
    Posting to a Friend's Timeline   67
The Settings Menu   68
Messages   69
Chatting on Facebook   71
The Poke   72

7

Introducing Twitter   73

What is Twitter?   73
What is a Tweet?   73
The 140 Character Tweet Limit   74
Followers   75
Direct Messages   75
Twitter and Photos   76
Profile Information   77
The Twitter Search Bar   78
Hashtags   78
Some of the Main Features of Twitter   79
    @   79
    Activity   79
    Direct Message (DM)   79
    Discover   79
    Favorite   79
    Follow   79
    Hashtag   79
    Mentions   80
    Notifications   80
    Profile   80

Reply 80
Retweet (RT) 80
Timeline 80
Trends 80
Tweet 80

8

Getting Started With Twitter 81
Introduction 81
Installing the Twitter App 81
Signing Up 82
Following Friends and Contacts 83
Inviting Friends to Join Twitter 84
Suggestions 85
Unfollowing Someone 86
Creating Your Profile 87
Editing an Existing Profile 88
A Tour of Twitter 90
Signing Out of Twitter 93
Android Tablet 93
iPad 94
Windows Tablet 94

9

Posting and Receiving Tweets 95
Introduction 95
Finding Someone on Twitter and Following Them 95
Posting a Tweet 96
Responding to Tweets 97
Replying to a Tweet 99
Receiving a Reply 100
Favorites 100
Viewing Images in Tweets 101
Android and iPad 101
Retweeting 102

Using@RTusername   102
Deleting Tweets   102
Hashtags   103
Trends   103
Key Facts: Posting and Receiving Tweets   104

10

Putting Photos Onto Your Tablet   **105**
Introduction   105
Using a Tablet's Built-in Cameras – Android   106
    Switching Between Front and Rear Cameras   106
    Selecting Photo or Video Mode   106
    Taking a Photo   107
    Making a Video   107
    Viewing Photos and Videos   107
Using the Built-in Cameras on an iPad   108
Viewing Photos and Videos on an iPad   109
More on the Camera Roll — Android and iPad   109
Importing Photos to a Tablet — Android   110
    Connecting a Digital Camera   110
    Connecting an SD Card Using a Card Reader   111
    Connecting a Micro SD Card   111
    Connecting a USB Flash Drive   111
    Transferring the Photos   112
    Accessing Photos on a Micro SD Card   112
Importing Photos to an iPad   113
Importing Photos to a Windows Tablet   114
    Using the Built-in Cameras   114
    Switching Between Front and Rear Cameras   114
    Connecting a Camera, Card Reader or Flash Drive 114
    Transferring the Photos   114
Managing Android and iPad Files Using a PC   115
Cloud Computing   116

Index   **117**

Introduction

What is Social Networking?

This is a method of communication between people over the Internet, which has developed rapidly over the last few years. It's much more versatile than previous methods, such as text messaging and e-mail, allowing communication in several different ways using various media.

Facebook is the largest social network, initially founded in 2004 at Harvard University. Since then, with the popularity of the Internet, it has spread around the world so there are now more than a billion users. Although Facebook was created primarily to help students to make friends and communicate with each other, it's now popular with people of all ages. This enables friends, families and colleagues to keep in touch using text, voice, photos and video, wherever they are in the world.

The Facebook Timeline

Twitter is the second most popular Social Network with hundreds of millions of users. As discussed in detail later, Twitter is used to post short text messages or *tweets* to anyone who chooses to follow you. Photographs may also be included.

The Twitter Profile and a Tweet

LinkedIn is a network aimed at professionals, enabling them to explore business and employment opportunities, but is beyond the scope of this book..

Uses of Social Networking

Social networking generally involves some or all of the following activities:

- Building a personal *profile* or *timeline*.
- Communicating with like-minded people.
- Sharing news and information in text messages.
- Creating albums and sharing photographs and videos.
- Chatting online and making voice and video calls.
- Promoting a business by posting news of latest events, product launches, etc.
- Following the posts of celebrities, journalists, etc.
- Gathering support for a cause or fund-raising event, etc.
- Taking part in online forums and debates.

Requirements for Social Networking

All you need to use Facebook or Twitter is a computer with an Internet connection and a valid e-mail address. There is no charge to use these websites — the companies make their money from advertising. Facebook states that users must be at least 13 years of age while Twitter doesn't specify an age limit.

Privacy and Security

When personal details are posted on websites like Facebook and Twitter, without suitable precautions, discussed later, the information may be accessible to a very large number of people. For example, care should be taken with address details and dates of holidays, for obvious reasons. Facebook allows users to restrict information to certain categories of user such as *Friends* or *Close friends*. The term 'friends' on Facebook simply means someone with whom you've agreed to exchange information, not necessarily a close personal friend who you know and trust.

Hardware Requirements

You can use any sort of computer for social networking, but obviously a portable, hand-held device like those listed below gives you the chance to communicate with others while you're in different situations and locations.

- The *smartphone*, a mobile phone with Internet and other computing capabilities and a screen size of up to approximately 5 inches, measured diagonally.
- The *phablet*, in between a smartphone and a tablet, with a screen size of about 5-7 inches.
- The *tablet*, a small hand-held computer with a typical screen size of 7-10 inches.

The tablet computer is ideal for social networking, having a good sized, easy to read screen. It is very light and can be held in one hand or carried in a small bag or large pocket.

Tablet Computers — An Overview

The explosion in the use of tablet computers in recent years has coincided with the increasing use of social networking websites.

The arrival of tablets such as the Apple iPad, the Google Nexus 7 and 10 and the Microsoft Surface have made it much easier to use social networking anywhere. The portability of tablets means they can be used wherever you can get a Wi-Fi signal or connect to a 3G or 4G mobile phone network. The tablet computer also makes it easy to use social networking in almost any situation — on a sofa, in bed, on a train, etc.

Although tablets are not ideal for the prolonged typing of long documents, this is not a problem with social networking. Facebook messages are usually very brief and Twitter places a limit of 140 characters on tweets.

The most successful single brand of tablet is the iPad, which has led the way in making hand-held computers so popular. There are now many other brands of tablets from companies such as Google, Asus, Sony and Samsung.

Tablets fall into three broad categories, based on the *Operating System (OS)*. This is the software used to control all aspects of a computer, apart from the current *application*, such as a game.

The three main tablet operating systems are:-

- **iOS**. The operating system used on the iPad range.
- **Android**. Google's operating system, used on tablets made by a variety of manufacturers.
- **Windows 8.1 and RT 8.1**. Used on the Microsoft Surface and other tablets. Various versions of Windows are also used on most laptop and desktop computers.

Versions of these operating systems are also used on smartphones and phablets.

iOS: The Apple iPad Operating System

This is used on the whole range of Apple tablets from the 7.9 inch iPad Mini up to the 9.7 inch iPad Air. The current version of the Apple operating system is iOS7, with iOS8 expected in 2014. The iPad pioneered a *touchscreen interface* with *icons* on the screen used to represent *applications* or *apps*, as they are known. Apps, previously known as *programs*, are the software needed for the activities you wish to pursue such as social networking with Facebook and Twitter. The screenshot below shows the icons for various apps on the iPad Home screen.

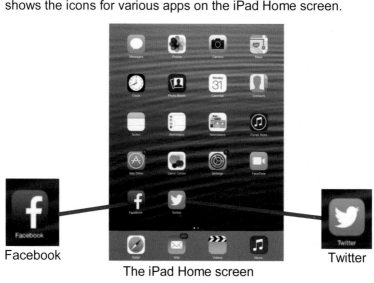

Facebook

Twitter

The iPad Home screen

The icons shown above are used to launch apps such as Facebook or Twitter. Tap the app with your finger or use a *stylus* — a pen-like device with a rubber tip, as shown on the right. Free apps for Facebook and

A touchscreen stylus

Twitter can be downloaded after tapping the App Store icon shown on the right. Then the apps are installed on the iPad with their own icons, as shown above.

Android: The Google Operating System

Android is used on more tablets and smartphones than any other operating system. Unlike iOS, which is only used on Apple products, Android is used on a large number of devices from many different companies such as Google, Asus, Samsung, Sony, Amazon, LG and Tesco.

The Standard Android OS

Tablets such as the Nexus 7 and 10 and the Tesco Hudl use the standard or stock version of Android, developed by Google from Linux, another popular computer operating system.

The Standard Android OS

Tweaked Versions of the Android OS

Android is known as an *open-source* operating system, meaning that you can modify the coding or instructions of the OS. So some companies supply tablets with their own 'tweaked' version of the Android OS, such as the Samsung Galaxy range and the Amazon Kindle Fire HDX.

The Samsung Galaxy version of Android uses a modified 'front-end' or user interface, known as *TouchWiz*, as shown below. Although somewhat different in layout and appearance, TouchWiz has many of the same features and icons as the standard Android and is operated in a similar way.

The Samsung Galaxy TouchWiz version of the Android OS

Free Android apps for Facebook and Twitter can be downloaded and installed from the Google Play Store, as discussed later.

Windows: The Microsoft Operating System

Microsoft Windows has been the dominant operating system on laptop and desktop computers for many years, with Windows XP and Windows 7 being two of the most popular versions. Windows 8 and Windows RT were launched in 2012 and introduced *touchscreen* operation for tablet computers alongside of the usual mouse and keyboard on laptop and desktop machines. Windows 8 can be used on tablet computers which have the standard x86 PC processor. This means tablets such as the Microsoft Surface Pro can run the huge catalogue of Microsoft Windows software used throughout the world. Windows 8 tablets are also produced by companies such as HP, Dell, Asus, Lenovo and Sony, in addition to Microsoft.

Windows RT is a special version of Windows 8, designed for tablet computers which use the ARM processor, such as the Microsoft Surface RT. Windows 8 and RT introduced a Start screen based on *tiles* rather than icons, as shown below. In 2013 Windows 8 and RT were superseded by Windows 8.1 and Windows RT 8.1. Tiles can be created for the apps for Facebook and Twitter, available from the Windows Store. These are shown below on the bottom right and on the next page.

The Start screen on Windows 8.1 and RT 8.1

As shown on the previous page, you can 'pin' tiles for Facebook and Twitter, (as shown below), to the Start screen on Windows 8.1 and RT 8.1. To start using Facebook or Twitter, just tap the appropriate tile.

The Windows 8.1 and RT 8.1 Apps Screen

If you prefer to launch apps from icons, rather than the Start screen, you can display all of your apps as icons, similar to the Home screens on the iPad and Android tablets discussed earlier.

When you install an app such as Facebook or Twitter from the Windows Store, an icon is automatically placed on the Apps screen, as shown below.

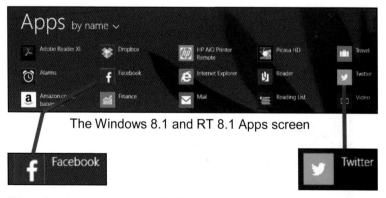

The Windows 8.1 and RT 8.1 Apps screen

Tiles for Facebook and Twitter should also be automatically placed on the Start screen as shown on page 8. If necessary, it's a simple task to create a tile on the Start screen for any app which appears on the Apps screen, as discussed in Chapter 2.

Social Networking on Different Platforms

As discussed earlier, most tablet computers use one of the three main operating systems or *platforms* — iOS, Android and Windows 8.1 (including RT 8.1). Special apps have been designed to run Facebook and Twitter on each OS. Although the three operating systems are different, the Facebook and Twitter apps are very similar on each OS, with the same icons and features but perhaps slightly different layouts, as shown below.

The Facebook Timeline

iPad
Operating system: iOS 7

Nexus 7
Operating system: Android

The Windows version of the Facebook app is also very similar to the iPad and Android versions shown above. The Twitter apps for all three tablet platforms also bear a close resemblance.

The fact that different brands of tablet have similar apps for Facebook and Twitter makes it simple to sign in and use these social networking sites on a variety of tablets. Where there are important differences between the apps for different platforms, these are explained in the appropriate parts of this book.

Getting Set Up

Connecting to the Internet

To use social networks like Facebook and Twitter you need a computer with a reliable Internet connection. If you are new to computing, you might think your tablet is faulty, when all that's needed is a quick re-connection to the Internet. Checking and, if necessary, restoring an Internet connection is discussed shortly.

There are several methods of making the connection, such as:

Wi-Fi

Using the *Wi-Fi* wireless technology built into the tablet to connect to the Internet via a *wireless router*.

3G or 4G (3rd or 4th Generation) SIM Card

Some tablets have a built-in slot for a *3G* or *4G SIM card*, to connect to the Internet via a mobile phone network. Alternatively use the Micro USB port on a tablet to plug-in a *mobile broadband dongle*. Or use a portable *Mi-Fi mobile hotspot* on the move to connect several Wi-Fi devices, such as tablets and laptops via a cell phone network.

Tethering

This involves connecting the tablet to a smartphone. The phone then acts like a router or mobile hotspot to connect the tablet to the Internet via the smartphone network.

You also need an e-mail address such as:

stellajohnson@gmail.com

Setting up an e-mail address is discussed shortly.

Wi-Fi

This often means connecting your tablet wirelessly to a *router* plugged into the telephone landline in your home. The necessary Wi-Fi technology is normally built into tablet and laptop computers. When you sign up for an Internet broadband service such as BT, Sky, Virgin or EE for example, a router may be included in the package. The router plugs into a spare telephone socket via a *filter*, which allows you to use the Internet at the same time as the phone. If necessary, an Internet service provider such as BT will send an engineer to set up the router. You can have several devices — tablets, laptops and desktop computers — all using one Wi-Fi router at the same time.

Wi-Fi Away from Home

There are now many places providing *wireless hotspots*, also known as *Internet access points*. These include hotels, restaurants and airports, etc. A tablet can detect and display a list of any available Wi-Fi networks in your current vicinity, including the one for your hotel or airport, etc., allowing you to connect to the Internet, as discussed shortly. If you need to enter a password, this should be provided by the establishment. The service may be free or there may be a small charge. Security may not be as good as on a home network.

BT Wi-Fi

If you subscribe to BT Broadband, you can have free access to over 5 million BT Wi-Fi hotspots in the UK and 7 million Fon hotspots overseas. The BT Hotspots are in popular hotels, restaurants and coffee shops, etc. If you do not subscribe to BT Broadband but want to use a tablet to access the Internet away from home, you can pay to use BT Wi-Fi. For short term use, you can buy hourly or daily vouchers while regular users can take out a monthly subscription.

Using a Wi-Fi Router

Connecting via a router in the home or via an Internet access point in a hotel or public place, etc., is probably the most economical way to get on the Internet. If you buy a 3G or 4G tablet to connect via a SIM card on the move, it should also have built-in Wi-Fi for connecting via a router.

The method for connecting to Wi-Fi is broadly the same for all types of tablet — iPad, Android or Windows 8.1 and RT 8.1.

First obtain the *network name* and the *wireless key* or *password*, if necessary, often printed on the back of the router.

Now open the Settings feature as shown below:

iPad

Tap the **Settings** icon on the Home Screen, shown on the right.

Android

Swipe down from the top right and tap **SETTINGS** from the small window that drops down. Shown below are the Settings icons for some of the main Android versions.

Jelly Bean (4.1-4.3)   KitKat (4.4)   Samsung TouchWiz

Windows 8.1 and RT 8.1

Swipe in from the right of the screen and tap the **Settings** charm as shown on the right.

Making the Connection

With the Settings window open, the method of connecting to a Wi-Fi network is very similar whatever tablet you are using. The following screenshots were taken using an iPad, but users of Android tablets should find them equally helpful. Extra notes for Windows 8.1 and RT 8.1 users are given on the next page.

Tap **Wi-Fi** and make sure it is **ON** by tapping or sliding the button, as shown in green below, near the top right.

You should see a list of networks, including your own. In our case it's the **BTHomeHub2-SW8N**. This name can be found on the back of the broadband router.

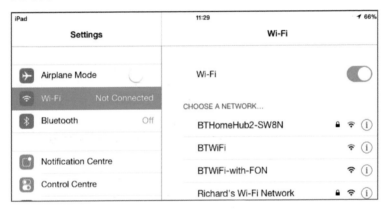

The networks shown above with a padlock icon, such as the **BTHomeHub**, are known as *secure networks* and require a password or wireless key to be entered.

The list of networks may include some networks belonging to your neighbours. Obviously you won't be able to log on to each other's secure networks without a password.

If necessary, enter the password for the network, as shown below.

Then tap **Join** or **Connect** to complete the process.

Once connected, a tick appears next to the network name, as shown above, or the word **Connected** is displayed. The information icon on the right and above displays technical details about the connection and an option to **Forget this Network** or **Join Network**.

Extra Notes for Windows 8.1 and RT 8.1

After tapping the **Settings** charm, the **Change PC settings** panel opens. Tap the **Available** icon shown on the right and then select your network from the list of available networks which is displayed. Tap the **Connect** button and the word **Connected** should appear below the network name, as shown below.

Checking Your Wi-Fi Connection

It's not unusual to lose your Internet connection and therefore not be able to access websites like Facebook and Twitter However, a faulty connection can usually be restored easily, as discussed on page 17. Wi-Fi icons, as shown below, enable you to see at a glance if you are connected to the Internet.

iPad

When connected, a Wi-Fi icon, as shown on the right, appears at the top left of the screen, as shown below.

Connected   Not connected

Android

On the Android range of tablets, the Wi-Fi icon appears in the Notification Area at the top right of the screen.

Connected   Not connected

Windows 8.1 and RT 8.1

The W-Fi icon appears in the Notification Area at the bottom right of the Windows Desktop and in the Settings area shown on page 15.

Connected   Not connected —   No connections
                 networks available   available

Weak Signal Strength

The Wi-Fi icons discussed on page 16 may be present but partially greyed out or faint, indicating a weak signal, as shown below. This may cause the Internet to work slowly or not at all.

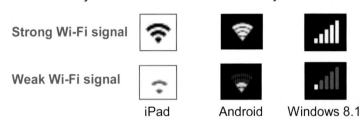

Strong Wi-Fi signal			
Weak Wi-Fi signal			
	iPad	Android	Windows 8.1

Other wireless devices nearby such as mobile phones may cause problems, so try moving them away. When using a tablet in a hotel, say, you may have a weak signal if your room is a long way from the router — try moving nearer to the router, if possible.

Restoring an Internet Connection

If you can't connect to the Internet and there is no Wi-Fi icon, (or a Windows 8.1 or RT 8.1 icon displays a cross), as discussed on the previous page, listed below are some possible remedies.

- Switch off and restart the router. This is a very common solution. Also restart the tablet if necessary.
- In Settings, as discussed on page 15, make sure **Wi-Fi** is switched **ON**. If necessary, select the network and enter the wireless key/password as described on page 15.
- Ensure that **Airplane Mode** (or **Flight mode**) is **OFF**.
- Check that the diagnostic lights on the router are correct according to the router manual.
- Remove and refit the detachable cables on the router.
- Also, when using Wi-Fi, in Settings make sure Bluetooth is **OFF**, as Bluetooth drains the tablet's battery very quickly.

3G or 4G SIM Card

Tablets with a Built-in SIM Card Slot

These are more expensive than a tablet with only Wi-Fi. The SIM card gives the tablet access to the Internet via a mobile phone network. As with a mobile phone, you can buy a SIM card and either pay upfront for a *data plan*, or take out a *contract*.

Mobile Broadband Dongle

The dongle looks similar to a memory stick and has a slot for a SIM card. The dongle plugs into the *Micro USB Port* on a tablet, via an *OTG* (On The Go) cable, as shown below on the right.

Mobile Broadband Dongle

OTG Cable

Mobile Broadband Hotspot

The mobile broadband dongle described above can only be used on one tablet at a time, via the single Micro USB port. A *mobile broadband hotspot* is a small, pocket-sized router that can be used to simultaneously connect several tablets or other devices to the Internet via a mobile phone network.

Like the other 3G/4G methods of connection above, a SIM card is required with either pay-as-you-go or a contract with the phone network.

Mobile Broadband Hotspot

The tablets, laptops, etc., connect to the hotspot using Wi-Fi, in this context also known as *MiFi* or *Mi-Fi*.

Tethering

In this method the tablet uses a smartphone as a router to access the Internet via the mobile phone network. The tablet is connected to the smartphone by one of the following methods:

Cable

The tablet and phone are connected by a USB cable.

Wi-Fi

In **Settings** on the phone, switch on **Portable Wi-Fi hotspot**. The tablet will detect the phone and show it in its list of available networks, enabling you to make the connection.

Bluetooth

This is wireless networking over short distances. With Wi-Fi **Off** and Bluetooth **On**, the tablet can search for and detect the phone. After *pairing* the two devices, the tablet can be connected to the Internet via the mobile phone network.

In the example below, a Nexus 7 tablet has searched for, detected and been paired with a Samsung Galaxy smartphone **GT-S6810P**. This allows the Nexus 7 to access the Internet via the Galaxy smartphone and, in this example, the EE mobile phone network.

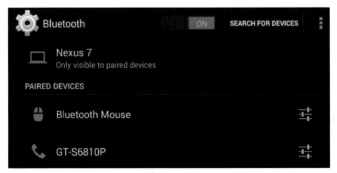

Nexus 7 tablet tethered to a Samsung Galaxy phone

Key Points: Wi-Fi vs 3G/4G

Wi-Fi

- If you plan to use a tablet mainly in the home or in hotels, airports, etc., where there are Wi-Fi Internet access points, a *Wi-Fi only* tablet will be all you need.

- A Wi-Fi only tablet will be cheaper than an equivalent tablet which also has a built-in 3G/4G SIM card slot.

- If you have a Wi-Fi only tablet, you can still use it for activities such as reading books on holiday in places where there is no Wi-Fi. Before leaving home, connect your tablet to the Internet using your router and download any books, music, etc., to the tablet's Internal Storage.

- With a Wi-Fi only tablet you will not be able to use Facebook or Twitter in places where there is no Wi-Fi.

3G/4G

- Using any of the 3G/4G methods described on pages 18-19 will require a pay-as-you-go *data plan* or a *contract* with a mobile phone company – probably more expensive than Wi-Fi using a router in your home, etc.

- A 3G/4G connection will allow you to connect to the Internet (and so use Facebook and Twitter) in places where there is no Wi-Fi. This means anywhere you can get a signal for the relevant mobile phone network.

Flight or Airplane Mode

- An airline may require you to switch on *Flight Mode* or *Airplane Mode* during a flight. This switches off the Internet and so you will not be able to access Facebook or Twitter, etc. (Although you can still access any previously downloaded music, photos, books, etc.)

Introducing the Web Browser

Once you're connected to the Internet you can launch your **web browser**, the app used for all your exploring of the Internet. It's essential to be familiar with your web browser and although there are several brands, they all work in a similar way. Some of the main browsers are Safari (iPad), Google Chrome (Android) and Internet Explorer (Windows 8.1 and RT 8.1).

Safari   Google Chrome   Internet Explorer

Open the web browser by tapping its icon on the Home screen. In the search bar, as shown below, enter keywords for a subject you wish to find out about. Alternatively enter the address of a web site, also known as the URL (Uniform Resource Locator).

After entering **www.facebook.com** into Google Chrome and tapping **Go**, the web page is displayed as shown below.

A Facebook web page displayed on an Android tablet

Similarly entering **www.twitter.com** into the search bar in Safari on an iPad opens the Twitter web site as shown below.

A Twitter web page displayed on an iPad

The Web Page Approach

The previous notes show that Facebook and Twitter are web sites which can be accessed by typing their web addresses into a browser. In fact this is was initially the standard way to use the two most popular social networking web sites on laptop and desktop computers. This web page approach is still popular with many people and is described in detail in our book *Social Networking for the Older Generation ISBN 978-0-85934-734-1*.

The App Approach

The tablet revolution has spawned a new type of software, i.e. programs, known as *apps*, specially designed for tablet computers. These are downloaded from an Internet *app store* and are either free or cost a few pounds. Millions of apps are available for tablets, such as Androids and iPads. Facebook and Twitter apps are available for the main brands of tablet and these are discussed in detail in the rest of this book. Once downloaded and installed the apps are launched by simply tapping their icons on the tablet's Home screen or Apps screen, as shown on the right.

Introducing Facebook

What is Facebook?

At the time of writing Facebook is the biggest social network, with well over a billion users around the world. Facebook is a Web site which allows anyone to create Web pages about themselves or their business and these can be viewed on any computer connected to the Internet, anywhere in the world. You just need a genuine e-mail address and the appropriate Facebook app for your tablet. You should also be at least 13 years of age.

Facebook apps are available for the three main types of tablet i.e. Android, iPad and Windows. These can be downloaded free from the appropriate apps store, i.e. the Play Store for Androids, the iPad App Store and the Windows Store. Once you've signed up for a Facebook account you can start exchanging information with people you choose to accept as Facebook friends. Signing up for a Facebook account is free — the company derives its income from advertisements. The advertising revenue is based on the *Click Through Rate* i.e. the number of times users of Facebook click (or tap on a tablet) on an advert to find out about a product or service. This chapter covers the following topics:

- What can you do with Facebook?
- Creating an e-mail account.
- Downloading the Facebook App.
- Signing up for Facebook.

What Can You Do With Facebook?

Listed below are some of the many Facebook facilities:

- Creating a network of contacts, known as *friends*, such as family, colleagues or customers. Invitations to become friends may be accepted or rejected.

- Providing an up-to-date personal *timeline* or *profile*. This includes information such as home address, telephone number and e-mail address.

- The profile can include details of your education and career and this may allow friends and colleagues from your past to contact you. If you include your interests, hobbies, likes and dislikes you may become a member of a Facebook *group* of like-minded people.

- You can include as much or as little information as you like in your profile and this can be edited or deleted at any time. *Audience selectors* can be used to control who can see your personal information.

- You can build up albums of photographs on your Facebook page, easily accessible to all your friends.

- Facebook includes text messaging, online 'chatting' and also photos, video clips and links to Web sites.

- Publicising future events or promoting a business. A group of friends with a common interest can join an online discussion or a campaign.

- Facebook provides access to third-party apps, i.e. software to do specific tasks, such as editing photographs or playing games.

Before Signing Up to Facebook

The requirements to sign up to Facebook are:

- A computer with an Internet connection.
- A valid e-mail address such as:
  johnsmith@gmail.com
- You must be at least 13 years of age.

The various methods of connecting a tablet computer to the Internet were discussed in Chapter 2.

Your E-mail Address

Your e-mail address is used as your login name every time you sign in to Facebook. You can't join Facebook unless you have a *genuine* e-mail address. When you first enter your e-mail address during the sign-up process (discussed shortly), any addresses which look false, comic or suspicious are rejected.

Security and Privacy

For security, a confirmation e-mail is sent to your e-mail address. You must respond to this e-mail before you can become a Facebook user. This is to ensure that only people with a genuine e-mail address can join Facebook. Facebook stores a great deal of personal information, giving the potential for misuse. However, very effective security measures are available and their use is strongly recommended, as discussed later.

Finding Friends

The list of contacts in your e-mail address book is used by Facebook to find people who may wish to become your friends. If you have more than one e-mail account, you can use several address books or contacts lists as the initial source of your potential Facebook friends.

Creating a New E-mail Address

If you already have an e-mail address, this can be used to sign up to Facebook. You've almost certainly created an e-mail address as part of the setting up process for a new tablet, such as Gmail on Androids, iCloud on the iPad and Mail on Windows.

However, you may wish to create a new e-mail address specifically for use with Facebook. In this case you can sign up for an account with one of the free e-mail services such as Google Mail, Yahoo! or Outlook.com, etc., as shown below.

Signing Up

A typical e-mail sign up process is shown below.

- Open the sign up page by entering e.g. **gmail sign up**, **Yahoo sign up**, or **Outlook sign up** in your browser, such as Google Chrome, Safari or Internet Explorer, etc.

- If necessary, select **Sign Up** or **Sign Up Now**.

- Complete the form as shown on the next page. Type the distorted letters (known as a *CAPTCHA*) to prove a human, not a computer, is completing the form.

- Agree to the terms of the e-mail service.

At the bottom of the screen, shown below, is the CAPTCHA, an acronym for Completely Automated Public Turing test to tell Computers and Humans Apart.

Installing the Facebook App

The app for Facebook may already be installed on your tablet, with an icon, as shown on the right, on the Home screen or Start screen and discussed on pages 5-8. If the icon is not present, the app can be downloaded free from the app store for your particular brand of tablet, as shown below.

iPad   Android   Windows

Tap the icon for your app store and then, in the **Apps** section of the store, enter **facebook** This is shown below in white text in the lime green search bar of the Android Play Store.

Tap the Facebook icon shown on the left above and then on the next screen tap **INSTALL** to place an icon for Facebook on your Home or Start screen.

The Facebook app is installed on iPad and Windows tablets in a similar way to that described above for Android tablets.

Signing Up For Facebook

Signing up for Facebook is broadly the same on all tablets, although there may be slight differences in the layout. Tap the Facebook icon on your Home or Start screen to launch the window shown below. Existing users simply enter their Facebook e-mail address and password in the two horizontal bars shown below, at the start of every Facebook session and tap **Log In**.

New users, i.e. those who've not yet got a Facebook account, should tap **Sign Up for Facebook**, as shown below.

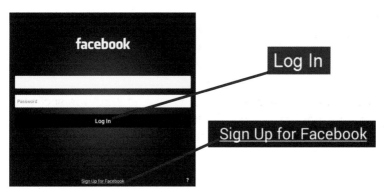

You are then required to enter the e-mail address you are going to use to log in to Facebook or if you need to reset the password. Facebook will check that this is a genuine e-mail address, as discussed shortly. Then tap **Continue**, as shown below.

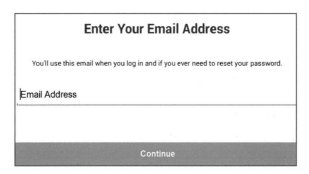

You are then asked to enter your first and last names. These should be your real name so that your friends can recognise you.

After tapping **Continue**, enter your password for Facebook, as shown below. This should have a combination of at least six numbers, letters and punctuation marks.

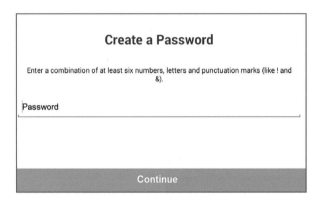

The next window allows you to select your birthday by scrolling the numbers on a calendar which pops up. Later on, if you prefer, you can hide your birthday from your profile.

> # What's Your Birthday?
>
> You can decide later if you want to hide your birthday from your profile. Learn More.
>
> Select Birthday

You are then asked to enter your gender. It's stated that providing this creates the best Facebook experience for you.

Tap **Continue** to open the **Add Your Photo** window shown below.

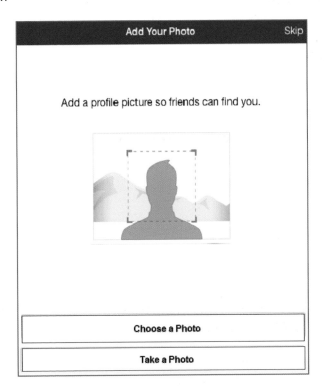

There are options to **Take a Photo** with your tablet or **Choose a Photo** in the **Gallery** on the tablet. However, you don't need to add your photo at this stage of the sign up process. The **Add Your Photo** window shown above has a **Skip** button, as shown on the top right above, allowing you to move on. You can change your profile, including your photo, at any time in the future when you are up and running with Facebook.

Taking photos with a tablet is discussed in detail later in this book. Also covered is transferring photos to a tablet from a stand -alone camera, for use in your Profile, Timeline or Updates.

Entering Your Profile Information

During the sign up process you are given the chance to start entering your profile, such as your education and employment details. This can be postponed until later by tapping **Skip** as shown below. Or tap **Save** if you do enter some of your details.

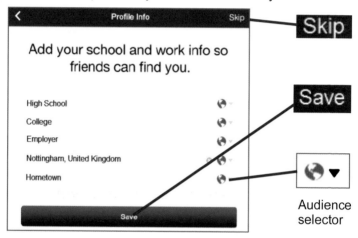

Audience
selector

Privacy — The Audience Selectors

The small icons at the right of each piece of data, as shown above and below, are used to protect your privacy. These *audience selectors* allow you to control who can see each piece of your data, such as **Public** (everyone) or just **Friends** or only **Close Friends**. This topic is discussed later.

Audience selector drop-down menu

You are then given the opportunity to find friends on Facebook, but this step can be postponed until later, if you prefer.

Confirming Your Account

The final step is to confirm that the e-mail address you have used to sign up to Facebook is really yours. Facebook send a confirmation code to the e-mail address, as shown below.

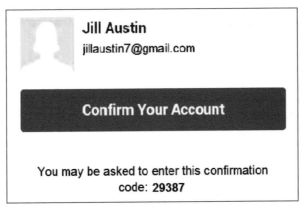

Check your e-mail Inbox to obtain the confirmation code. Then enter the code in the Facebook **Account Confirmation** window shown below.

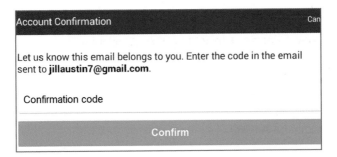

The sign up process is now complete and you should be able to **Log In** to Facebook and start building your social network.

Launching Facebook

Tap the Facebook icon on your Home or Start screen. One of the main screens you will be using is your *Timeline* or *Profile*, as shown below on an Android tablet (Nexus 7).

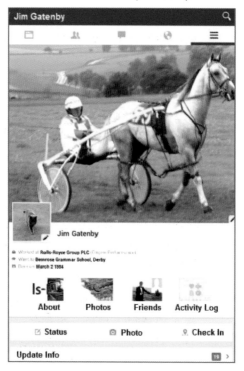

The main photograph at the top is your *Cover Photo*, selected from the *Gallery* on your tablet. The small picture on the lower left is your *Profile Picture*. The lines of small text beneath the Profile Picture are part of your Profile Info, such as your school, employment and date of birth. The lower part of the Timeline (not shown above) also includes a listing of the main events in your life from your birth onwards, as discussed in more detail later.

As discussed later, your Profile Information can be edited at any time and the privacy set using the *audience selectors*.

Facebook Features

Listed below and on the next page are some of the main Facebook features. These are described in more detail, with examples and screenshots, in the chapters which follow.

Applications   Usually known as *Apps* for short, these are programs or software on Facebook such as games or even the Facebook app itself.

Audience Selectors   Icons and menus used to control who can see your information. (Privacy settings).

Chat   This facility allows you to have a real-time conversation with friends by typing the words into a small window on the screen.

Comment   This enables you to type a short note in response to a status update or photograph.

Events   This feature allows you to inform friends about future events and social occasions.

Facebook   A worldwide social network with over a billion members, exchanging news and information, photographs and videos.

Friend   A person with whom you have agreed to exchange information on Facebook.

Friend request   An offer of friendship on Facebook which can be accepted, declined or ignored.

Group   This feature allows Facebook users to collaborate with other people sharing a common interest and to join online forums.

Home page   The Home page contains your News Feed and links to many other features such as Messages, Events and Friends.

Like   Tapping the *Like* icon next to an update or photo on the screen is a quick way to register your approval of an update or photo.

Message	A note sent to a particular friend or friends, similar to an e-mail. May include photos, etc.
News Feed	Part of your Home page, informing you of your friends' latest activities on Facebook.
Notifications	These are short messages which pop up on the screen telling you about something that happened on Facebook.
Page	Page in this context refers to a feature for businesses, organisations and celebrities, etc., to broadcast information to a wide audience.
Poke	This is a way of saying hello to a friend and reminding them you exist and are online.
Post	A status update, photo or video placed on your News Feed and also your friends' News Feeds, depending on the privacy setting.
Privacy Settings	Audience selector settings used to control who can see which parts of your Facebook information and photographs, etc.
Profile	Your Profile (Timeline) lists your personal information, photos, career and interests as well as posts stating what you and your friends have been doing.
Status Update	A short post to friends saying what you're doing, etc. A photo, video or Web link can be included. Friends can reply by writing a comment or tapping *Like*. The status update also appears on your own Timeline.
Tagging	Labelling a friend's name on a photo, so that other people can identify them.
Timeline	A listing of your Profile and your activities on Facebook, in chronological order, including photos, updates and posts from friends.

Building Your Profile

Introduction

As discussed in Chapter 3, you may have already entered some of your Profile information during the sign up process for Facebook. Or you may have tapped **Skip** to move on quickly, intending to enter the Profile information later. You can enter or, if necessary, edit the Profile information at any time, e.g. if your address or employment details change.

Tap the Facebook icon on your Home or Start screen and log in to Facebook as discussed earlier. Tap the 3 bar icon shown on the right and below on an Android tablet. Then tap your name to open your Timeline.

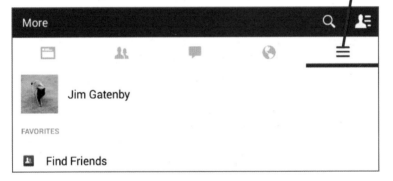

After tapping your name, the Timeline opens as shown on page 34. On an Android tablet, tap **Update Info** as shown below and on the bottom left of the screenshot on page 34.

On the iPad, tap the 3 bar icon and then tap your name, as before. Then tap in the panel on the Timeline displaying your work and school, etc., as shown on the screenshot below. Your Profile should now appear.

Alternatively, on tablets in general, tap on the **About** button shown on the left and on the left above. Then tap **About** again or **More about…** to see your full Profile.

You are now ready to start completing your Profile, as shown on the next page.

Use the *audience selectors* to keep private any information you wouldn't post on a public noticeboard.

Apart from basic details such as your school, contact details and employers, you can also enter details of your interests and professional skills, etc. Scroll the form upwards to enter more information about yourself, such as your favourite quotation, relationship status or simply write something you want to say about yourself. This should help you to make friends with people having similar backgrounds, experience and interests.

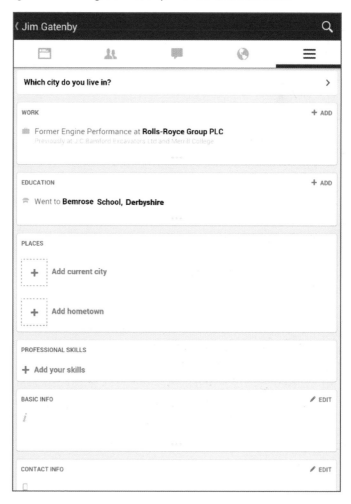

Entering and Editing Profile Information

You may need to tap **View Profile** or **More About ...** to see the entire Profile. Tap the item of information you wish to enter or edit. If necessary, scroll up to see the lower items of information, as shown in the extract below.

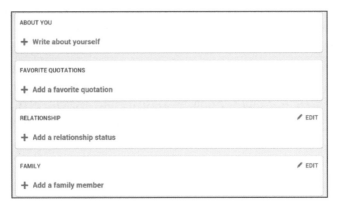

Tap in a horizontal information slot and enter or edit the information, as shown below. Then tap the *audience selector* icon shown on the left. Finally select the level of privacy you require from the drop-down menu shown below.

Protecting Your Privacy

It's really important to use the privacy settings in Facebook to ensure that your personal information such as **CONTACT INFO** only reaches your intended audience. Anyone on Facebook can type your name in the Facebook search bar and find your Profile. Without adequate security they might find where you live, when you are going to be away from home and lots of other sensitive information.

The drop-down audience selector menu can be extended by tapping on **...More Options** shown at the bottom of the previous page. This adds further options to restrict the viewing of a piece of information to **Only Me** or **Close Friends**, as shown below.

As discussed later, anyone can find you and invite you to be a Friend on Facebook, including people you don't know and may not be able to trust.

Finally tap **Save** shown above on the right to permanently record the new or edited information.

Pieces of information with privacy set at **Public** can be viewed by anyone and everyone.

Finding and organising Friends is discussed shortly

Uploading a Profile Picture
Android and iPad

This is the thumbnail picture on the left of the Timeline, as shown on page 38 featuring Bop the cat. It should really be a picture of yourself, to identify you to your friends on any updates you send, especially if many people have the same name as you.

When you start entering your Profile information, the thumbnail space is initially blank. To upload a photo for the first time or to change or edit an existing Profile Picture, tap in the small, thumbnail image area shown here on the right and on page 38.

The small menus shown below appear.

Edit Profile Picture	View Profile Picture
View Photo	Upload Photo
Android	iPad

If you tap **Edit Profile Picture** or **Upload Photo** you are presented with a display of the photos saved on your tablet, from which you can choose your new Profile Picture. The iPad screen below is very similar to the Photos screen on Android tablets.

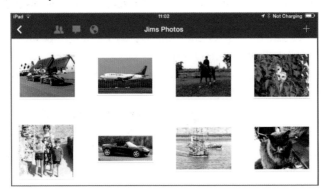

Tap on a photo as shown on the previous page and the photo opens as shown below, allowing you to **Move** or **Scale** the image. For example, you might want to move an image to centralise it in the available space.

Move and Scale

Cancel   Done

Android

When you tap **Done**, as shown above for the Android, the picture is uploaded to Facebook as your new Profile Picture. On the iPad, the **Move** and **Scale** screen is very similar, but the **Done** button is very small and at the top right of the screen.

The Timeline with the new owl Profile Picture uploaded to Facebook is shown below.

When you tap **View Photo** or **View Profile Picture**, after tapping on a Profile Picture, as shown on the previous page, the image is displayed on the full-screen as shown below.

Android

Tapping the Android 3 dot menu shown on the right and above displays the menu shown on the left below. The iPad has a horizontal 3 dot menu, shown on the right, which opens the menu shown on the right below.

Android

iPad

Make profile picture
Make cover photo
View album
Edit caption
Delete photo

Android

Delete Photo
Save Photo
Share

iPad

Windows 8.1 and RT 8.1 Tablets

The method of changing the Profile Picture on Windows tablets is broadly similar to that just described for Android and iPad tablets Tap the Profile Picture on the left of the Timeline, as shown at the bottom of page 43, in this case the picture of a little owl. The menu shown below appears.

	View Profile Picture
	Take Photo
	Choose From Library
	Set Windows Account Picture

Windows Tablets

View Profile Picture produces the full-screen picture shown on page 44, with a horizontal 3 button menu icon, also shown on page 44.

Take Photo allows you to use the camera on your tablet to take a new **Profile Picture**.

Choose From Library is used to select a new Profile Picture from those in your tablet's Internal Storage.

All Tablets

Taking photos using the in-built cameras on your tablet and saving them on the Internal Storage on the tablet is discussed in more detail in Chapter 10. Also described is the copying of photos to the Internal Storage of your tablet, from external devices such as stand-alone digital cameras, SD and Micro SD camera cards and USB flash drives.

Changing the Cover Picture

The Cover Picture is the large photograph across the top of your Timeline, as shown on page 38. Tap anywhere on the Cover Picture area then, on Android or iPad tablets, select either **Change Cover** or **Upload Photo** from the small menu which appears, as shown below.

Android   iPad

Then browse and select a photo to upload as your new Cover. The iPad also has a camera icon, shown on the right, to take a new Cover Photo using the in-built camera on the iPad.

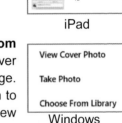

iPad

On Windows tablets the option **Choose From Library** can be used to select the new Cover Photo from the tablet's Internal Storage. Alternatively, there is a **Take Photo** option to use the tablet's own camera to take a new Cover Photo.

View Cover Photo

Take Photo

Choose From Library

Windows

After tapping the photo to be uploaded, the new cover can be previewed and saved, as shown in the Android example below.

Finding Friends

Introduction

The term *friends* on Facebook covers all the people you communicate with; this includes members of your family and colleagues from work and perhaps your student days, as well as close personal friends. It may also include people with whom you share a common interest. You can invite people to be your friend and they can accept or reject the invitation.

There are various methods used by Facebook to help you find people who you might want as friends, such as:

Suggestions

From your profile information, Facebook suggests people having something in common with you, such as your home district, school, college or employer.

Search

You can enter someone's name or e-mail address into the search bar in Facebook. Then send a friend request.

Requests

You may receive requests to 'friend' someone who has seen your Profile or perhaps knows you from previous times.

Contacts

You can invite people who are in your list of e-mail contacts or friends of friends on Facebook.

Browse

This allows you to search for people from your school, college, employment and interests, etc., to invite as friends.

Finding Friends — iPad and Android

The next four pages describe the methods of finding friends on iPad and Android tablets. Finding friends using Windows 8.1 tablets is discussed on page 52.

After launching Facebook, tap the 3 bar icon and then tap **Find Friends,** as shown below.

The **Find Friends** window opens, displaying buttons to find people to invite to be friends, as shown below.

Suggestions

Tapping **Suggestions** shown on the left above displays a list of people who Facebook suggests you may want as friends, based on your profile and contacts through e-mail and mutual friends. Tap **Add Friend** against their name to send an invitation.

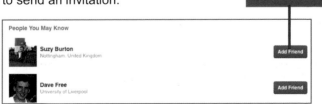

Search

The **Search** option shown below allows you to enter the name or e-mail address of someone you would like to have as a friend on Facebook.

If the person already has a Facebook account, they will automatically be sent a request to be your friend. Any requests you receive can be displayed by tapping the **Requests** button shown on the right and below. Then tap **Confirm** or **Delete**, as shown below.

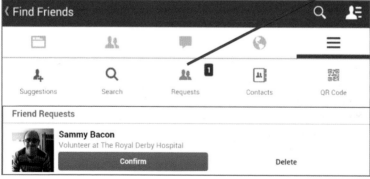

If the person doesn't have a Facebook account an invitation to join Facebook will be sent to their e-mail address.

Contacts   iPad and Android

Facebook provides a list of all the people you correspond with by e-mail or who are friends of your friends who are already on Facebook.

Tap the **Contacts** button shown below to select one of your e-mail services and sign in to your account.

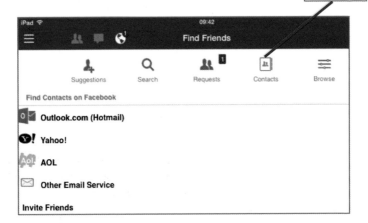

Then tap the **Invite** buttons as shown below to ask any of your contacts, who are members of Facebook, to be your friend.

Any of your e-mail contacts who are not members of Facebook are sent an invitation to join, as shown at the bottom of page 54.

Browse

iPad and Android

Tap the **Browse** button shown on the right and below. This displays a list of your previous places of work and education, etc.

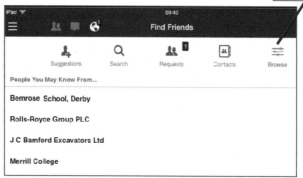

Now select one of the organisations in which you have been involved at some time. Facebook responds with a list of people from that organisation who are members of Facebook.

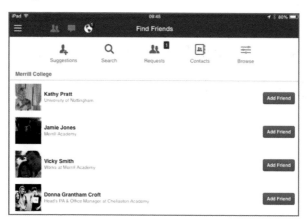

Tap the **Add Friend** button next to the name of anyone you want to be your friend on Facebook, as shown above. Once they've accepted your invitation they will appear in your list of Friends.

Finding Friends — Windows 8.1 and RT 8.1

As mentioned on page 48, the Windows tablets use a different screen layout for finding friends, although the basic methods are the same.

Tap your name on the top left of the Facebook screen to display your Timeline, as shown below. Then tap the **Activity Log** button, shown on the right and below.

Activity Log

The Activity Log opens as shown below, in this case recording the fact that my Profile Picture had been changed to feature our latest cat, obtained from the local rescue centre. At the top of the Activity Log is a **Find Friends** button shown on the right and below.

Windows 8.1 and RT 8.1

The **Find Friends** feature in the Windows 8.1 and RT 8.1 app presents a list of people you may know, for example, people who are friends of your existing Facebook friends. Tap **Add Friend** to send them a friend request.

Down the right-hand side of the page above are a number of boxes enabling you to select sources from your Profile to search for potential friends. These might include your schools, colleges, universities, employers and mutual friends.

The Facebook app for tablets using Windows 8.1 and RT 8.1 has the usual facility to search your contacts such as those from your e-mail address book(s). After tapping **Find Friends**, shown in the left window below and on the top right of the main screenshot on the previous page, you can import your e-mail contacts to Facebook and send them invitations to be friends.

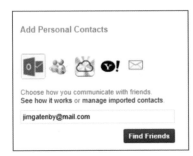

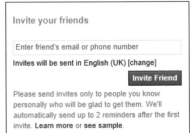

All Tablets

The window on the right above or similar on Androids and iPads is used to invite individual friends to join Facebook. After entering your friend's e-mail address and tapping **Invite Friend**, an e-mail is sent, as shown in the sample below. Your contact could then tap **Join Facebook** if they wished. Facebook also sends up to two reminders if people don't respond to the initial invitation.

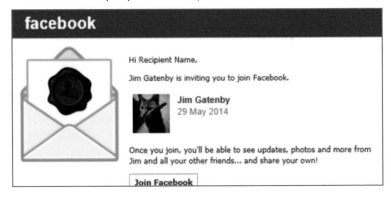

Managing Friends   All Tablets

Friend Lists

A major part of Facebook is the posting of *status updates* giving news and information to your friends and family, etc. These can include photos and videos, etc., and are discussed in more detail shortly. By arranging your friends into *lists*, such as **Family** and **Close Friends**, you can target your updates at specific groups of people, using *audience selectors* as discussed shortly.

Adding Friends to a List

Tap **Friends** on the left of the screen to see a list of your friends, as shown below.

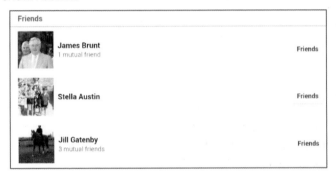

Tap the name of a friend, as shown above, to open the friend's Timeline, as shown below.

On Android and iPad tablets, tap the **Friends** button under the Cover Picture on your friend's Timeline, as shown on the right and on the previous page.

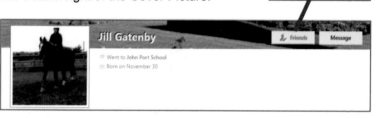

On Windows tablets the Friends button is on the bottom right of the Cover Picture.

Edit Friend Lists — Android

After tapping the Friends button, Android tablets open the **Edit Friend Lists** window shown below. Tap against a list, such as **Close Friends** or **Family**, to add the selected friend to that particular list, indicated by a tick.

Unfollow and **Unfriend** shown above are discussed shortly.

Edit Friend Lists — iPad and Windows

After tapping the appropriate **Friends** button as shown at the top of the previous page, a small menu appears, as shown below.

| iPad | Windows 8.1 and RT 8.1 |

Tap **Edit Friend Lists** shown above to open the window shown below.

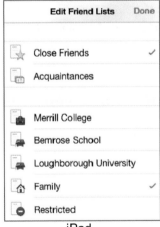

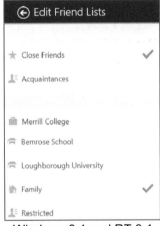

| iPad | Windows 8.1 and RT 8.1 |

You can now use the lists in your *audience selectors* to make available your posts to certain people or to read their latest posts.

The screenshots above and at the bottom of page 56 show that the versions of the Facebook app for Android, iPad and Windows tablets are basically the same, although different in appearance.

The following terms relate to the Friend Lists on the previous two pages and apply to Android, iPad and Windows tablets.

Acquaintances

The **Acquaintance** list is for friends you don't need to keep in close touch with. You can exclude them from a post using the audience selector **Friends Except Acquaintances**.

Restricted

If you put someone on your **Restricted** list as shown on pages 56 and 57, they will only see your updates and photos if the audience is set at **Public**. If you set the audience as **Friends**, people on the **Restricted** list won't see your update or photos.

Unfriend

Tapping **Unfriend** as shown in the screenshots on pages 56 and 57 removes a person from your friend list and you are removed from theirs.

Unfollow

Followers can see your posts in their News Feed. You can set your account to allow Everyone (**Public**) or only **Friends** to follow you. From your Home Page select **Account Settings** or **Settings** then **Followers**. You automatically follow your friends and you can follow anyone else if they set **Followers** to **Public**. To follow someone tap **Follow** on their Timeline. If someone doesn't allow following, the **Follow** button doesn't appear on their Timeline. Tap **Unfollow** as shown on pages 56 and 57 to stop following someone.

Blocking

This stops people seeing your posts on your Timeline, inviting you to events and adding you as a friend, amongst other things.

Select **Account Settings** or **Settings** then tap **Blocking**. Enter the name or e-mail address of the person then tap **Block**.

Using Facebook

Introduction

Earlier chapters looked at the setting up of a new Facebook account and the entry of information about yourself in your Profile, part of your Timeline. The previous chapter showed how to search your e-mail contacts lists and elsewhere for people to invite to become your Facebook friends. These people may accept or reject your invitation. This chapter shows how you can start to use Facebook to communicate with friends.

Signing In

Tap the Facebook icon on your Apps screen or, on Windows tablets, tap the tile on the Start screen. Then enter your e-mail address and password in the Log In window shown below.

After you tap the **Log In** button, shown above, Facebook displays your **News Feed**, shown on the next page. Your News Feed displays your recent Facebook activity and any exchanges of information between you and your friends. These exchanges are known as *status updates* or *posts*.

Navigating Around Facebook

The News Feed

As shown below, the News Feed displays copies of the *Status Updates* that you post. The Status Update, also known simply as a *Status* or an *Update*, can contain text, photos, videos and links to websites and is discussed in more detail shortly.

Menu button

iPad News Feed

On an iPad, tap the 3 bar menu button shown on the left above, to display the Facebook menu shown below. (On an Android tablet, the 3 bar menu button is on the top right of the screen).

Your name

iPad Menu

Android and Windows tablets have a similar Facebook menu down the left-hand side of the screen.

The Timeline

The Timeline shows your Profile and major events in your life, in chronological order. The Timeline includes the updates that you post and changes to your Profile or Profile Picture, for example. To display your Timeline, tap your name at the top of the menu shown at the bottom of page 60. To open a friend's Timeline, tap **Friends** on the menu shown on page 60 then tap their name on your Friends list, such as **Stella Austin**, shown below.

You can view the Timelines of people who are on Facebook, but who are not your friends, after entering their name in the Facebook search bar. However, how much you see depends on the audience selector settings used by the owner of the Timeline.

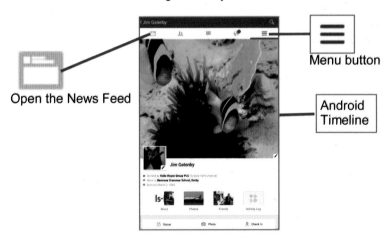

To return to the News Feed from the Timeline, tap the small **News Feed** icon near the top left of the screen, as shown on the right and on the left above.

Posting a Status Update

The Status Update is used to tell other people your latest news, where you are and what you're doing and to share photos and videos.

Posting an Update from the Timeline

On an Android or Windows tablet tap **Status** on the Timeline, as shown below on the left, to open the Update Status or Write Post window shown on the next page. On an iPad tablet tap **Write Post** on the Timeline, as shown below on the right.

Android and Windows   iPad

Posting an Update from the News Feed

All three types of tablet, Android, iPad and Windows have a menu bar on their News Feed, which has icons called **Status**, **Photo** and **Check In**, as shown below for the iPad.

Tap **Status** on the News Feed to open the Update Status or Write Post window shown on the next page.

Writing a Post or Status Update

The window in which you write an update is shown below, for an Android, where it is called **Write Post**. On iPad and Windows tablets it's called the **Update Status** window. However, the versions of the window for Android, iPad and Windows are very similar. The on-screen keyboard pops up when the window is opened, ready for you to start typing the text of your update, replacing the words **What's on your mind?**

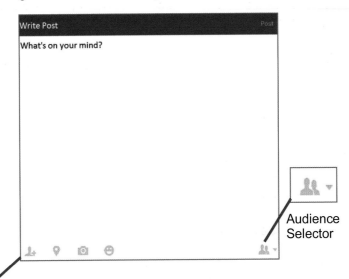

Audience
Selector

The icons on the left above have the following functions:

 Add who you're currently with. Suggestions from within your friends are provided by Facebook.

 Say where you are. A list of local places is provided.

 Insert in the update a photo stored on your tablet. (Working with photographs is discussed in detail later in this book).

 Say what you're currently doing. This feature includes suggestions, such as Feeling, Eating, Travelling, etc.

The Audience Selector

To control who can see an update, tap the *audience selector* icon shown on the right and on page 63. The **Audience** or **Share With** menu opens, as shown below, for Android and iPad. The Windows menu is very similar.

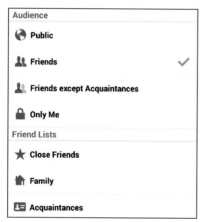

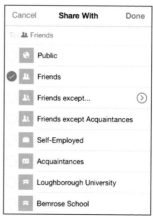

| Android | iPad |

When you tap a category such as **Friends** above, it is marked with a tick. **Acquaintances** are **Friends** that you don't expect to be in contact with very often. So they can be excluded from a post by ticking **Friends except Acquaintances**, as shown above.

Posting

After you've have finished creating the update, tap **Post** at the top right of the **Update Status** (or **Write Post**) window.

The new update appears on your Timeline and your News Feed. It also appears on the News Feeds of the Friends you've included in the audience selector, as described above.

Please Note: Selecting **Public**, i.e. Everyone, on an update, allows *anyone* to find you on Facebook and view the update.

Shown below is an update which Jill had posted to her friends. The photo of the Jay was taken with a separate digital camera and uploaded to an iPad, as discussed in Chapter 10.

If you tap **Like**, shown above, the thumbs up sign is highlighted in blue. The number of **Likes** appears on the copy of the update on the originator's News Feed. Tap this to see who liked the update.

Tapping **Comment** above opens a window in which you can write a response to the post.

Share above allows you to post a copy of the update to friends' Timelines, your own Timeline or to a Facebook Group.

Posting a Web Link in a Status Update

If you think your friends may be interested in a particular Web site, you can send a live *link* or *hyperlink* as part of a status update. Tap **Status** or **Write Post** in your Timeline or News Feed to open the **Write Post** or **Update Status** window shown below and on page 63. Then enter the address of the website you wish to share, together with a message, as shown below.

Use the audience selector to control who will see the post, as discussed on page 64. In this case an individual friend, **Jill** has been selected. Then tap the **Post** button shown above and the link soon appears on the News Feed(s) of your friend or friends, as shown below, together with your text message.

Friends can then tap the link to open the website, in this example **www.babanibooks.com**, in their web browser, such as Google Chrome, Apple Safari or Microsoft Internet Explorer.

Posting to a Friend's Timeline

From your own Timeline select **Friends** and then tap the name of your friend in the list of friends which appears. This opens the friend's Timeline as shown below.

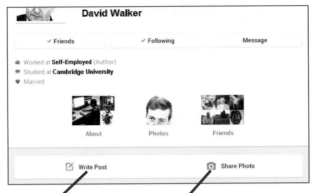

Then tap **Write Post**, or **Share Photo** on your friend's Timeline and write the text and insert any pictures, etc., as described on pages 63 and 64. Then tap the **Post** button and the update soon appears on your friend's Timeline, as shown below.

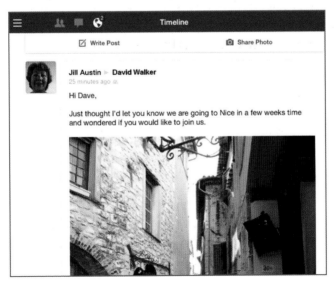

The Settings Menu

The **Settings** menu, also known as **Account Settings**, has many functions such as **Blocking** friends and controlling who can see what you and others post on your Timeline.

On Android and iPad tablets, launch Facebook and tap the 3 bar menu shown on the right and on page 60 and 61. Then select **Settings** or **Account Settings** from the main menu down the left-hand side of the screen, as shown on page 60. The **Settings** window opens, as shown below.

On Windows 8.1, from Facebook swipe in from the right and tap the **Settings** charm. Then tap **Account Settings** in the right-hand panel to launch the **Settings** window.

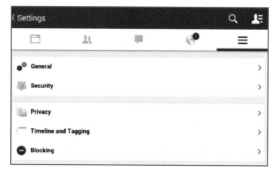

For example, if you tap **Timeline and Tagging** shown above and then **Who can see what others post on your timeline?**, you can tap to select, with a tick, one of the audiences shown below.

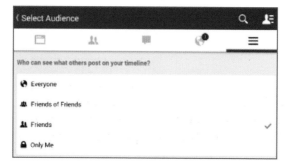

Messages

This feature is different from the Status Updates just described. The Update is posted to your Timeline and your News Feed and to the News Feeds of your friends. Depending on your privacy settings discussed earlier, other people can find your name on Facebook and read the updates on your Timeline.

A *message*, on the other hand, is sent to one or more people, like an e-mail and can be used for a private conversation. Other people will not be able to see it.

On Android and iPad tablets, the Messages feature can be opened by tapping the icon shown on the right and below.

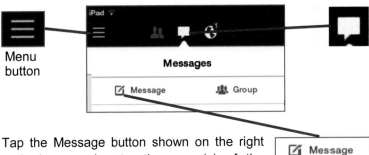

Menu
button

Tap the Message button shown on the right and above and enter the name(s) of the recipient(s) of the message in the **To:** bar, as shown below.

Alternatively, on Apple and Windows tablets, tap the 3 bar menu button shown on the left above, then tap **Messages** on the menu down the left-hand side of the screen. Then tap the New Message icon shown on the right.

Enter the text of the message in the bar at the bottom of the **New Message** window, as shown below.

To include a photo, tap the paperclip icon, shown above. As shown below, you can insert a photo from your tablet or take or a new one. You can also add a *sticker* or image as shown below.

Tapping the blue arrow head shown above inserts your *location* in the message. When your message is finished, tap **Send**, as shown on the right.

Your recipient receives the message, as shown below on

the left. Tapping the message displays the photo, as shown on the right below and allows the recipient to start a conversation by entering a reply.

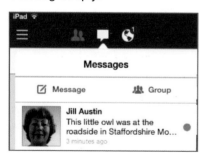

Chatting on Facebook

Chat allows two or more online Facebook friends to exchange messages in real time. Your messages appear on your contact's screen immediately, allowing them to send an instant reply.

On an iPad, to check that Chat is turned on, turn the tablet horizontal and tap the gear icon shown on the right, on the top right of the News Feed. If necessary tap **Turn On Chat**.

On an Android tablet, tap the icon shown on the right, on the right of the News Feed. Then tap the gear icon and make sure **Chat** is turned on with a tick. On Windows the Chat gear icon is at the bottom right of the screen.

| iPad | Android |

A green spot against a friend's name above shows they are online and able to start a conversation. Tap the friend's name to open the Chat window and start exchanging messages, writing alternately in their respective New Message windows, as shown below.

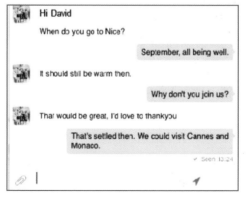

Facebook Chat

The Poke

This is a quick way to say hello to someone and to let them know you exist and are still on Facebook. Tap the 3 bar menu button and select **Pokes** from the main menu. Then enter the name of the friend in the Search bar and tap **Yes**, as shown below.

Alternatively, from your **Friends** list, tap your friend's name to open their Timeline. Then tap the **Poke** icon at the top right of their Timeline and tap **Poke** from the drop-down menu.

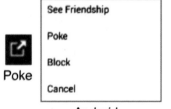

Poke   Poke

Android   iPad

The person receiving the poke may see a *Notification*, as shown on the right, which they tap to open the poke. Or they can tap **Pokes** on their main menu. They can then tap **Poke Back** if they wish to reply. Tap **Block** shown above to stop any further pokes from the friend.

Introducing Twitter

What is Twitter?

This chapter gives an overview of Twitter and what it's used for. Later chapters give more detailed instructions about setting up a Twitter account and how to use it.

Like Facebook, Twitter is a social network, allowing people to communicate and interact over the Internet. Twitter is the second most popular social network behind Facebook and has millions of users, posting hundreds of millions of *tweets* a day.

What is a Tweet?

A tweet is a short text message, as shown below, which can be immediately viewed by an audience of thousands or even millions of people — if you're a celebrity or well-known person.

james gatenby @jim gatenby
Recently adopted a cat from the rescue centre. Very nervous at first but now very bossy. Delights in knocking small objects onto the floor.

However, lots of ordinary people use Twitter to tell their friends and families what is happening in their lives. Many Web sites representing companies and organisations include a link to their Twitter pages where you can read their latest news. Celebrities and people with a lot of followers can use Twitter to get their message out to a wide audience. Twitter can also be used to host a debate or to marshal support for a charitable cause.

Latest News

Some of the essential features of Twitter are:

- Tweets, i.e. messages, can be up to 140 characters.
- Tweets are posted onto the Home page of *followers*.
- Apart from text, a tweet can include a link to a photograph, video or a Web site.

The 140 Character Tweet Limit

The SMS text messages used on mobile phones were an influence on the creators of Twitter. It was thought that by enforcing a limit of 140 characters, 'tweeters' would be more concise and organise their thoughts better — "brevity is the soul of wit". If you try to enter more than 140 characters, the message is truncated. You don't have to use the full 140 characters if you don't need to. The number **27** on the bottom right below is the number of characters available before the limit is reached. The contents of a tweet can be anything you like as long as it's not offensive, in which case the tweet may be removed.

Cancel	**New Tweet** james gatenby (@jimgatenby)	Tweet
Just saw an Andropov 225, the world's biggest aircraft. Six engines and nearly as big as a football pitch.		
◙ ♀		27

The tweet appears on your Home page and on the Home pages of the people following you. Creating a tweet can include the insertion of links to photographs, videos and Web sites. These topics are discussed in more detail in Chapter 10.

Followers

Twitter is based on the concept of *followers.* A follower is someone who is interested in reading someone else's tweets. Although celebrities can have millions of followers, you could equally have a small group of friends or relatives following each other. When you post a tweet it appears almost immediately on the Home pages of all your followers. A link at the bottom of a tweet allows followers to post a reply. The followers of important people or celebrities may simply want to read the tweets out of interest, without expecting to take part in a two way conversation.

A small group of friends or family all online on Twitter, might post immediate replies. You can also *retweet* or forward someone else's tweet to the people following you.

Normally when you post a tweet, anyone can see it after searching for your name. It's possible to set the privacy so only your approved followers can see the tweet, as discussed later.

Twitter allows you to search for people by name or by their e-mail address and then start following them or you can invite friends to join Twitter via e-mail. Twitter also displays a list of celebrities you may wish to follow. You can choose who you want to follow, but you can't choose who follows you. You can *unfollow* someone you no longer wish to follow.

Direct Messages

Normally when you create a tweet it is sent to all of the people who are following you. On the other hand, *direct messages* are sent to a particular person who is following you.

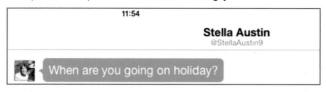

Direct Messages are discussed in more detail in Chapter 8.

Twitter and Photos

A tweet can include a link to a file such as a photograph, as shown below. You can also insert links to videos and Web sites.

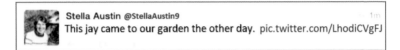

When someone reads the tweet, they can click on the blue link **pic.twitter.com/LhodiCVgFJ** shown above to open the full image. Or tap the text of the tweet to display both the tweet and the photo as shown below.

Icons along the bottom right of the tweet, as shown above, allow you to reply to the tweet, mark it as a **FAVORITE** or **RETWEET** it to someone else.

Inserting photos into tweets is discussed in detail in Chapter 10.

Profile Information

As discussed in more detail later, you can create a *Profile* for yourself or your business.

The profile information appears along the top of the Twitter page as shown above.

The Profile Photo

The is the small image and can be up to 3MB in size.

The Header Photo

You can also include a Header photo of up to 5MB. This is the wide picture across the top of the screen shown above. Up to 160 characters of text are allowed, a location to say where you are and a link to a web site.

Creating and editing your Profile is discussed in more detail in Chapter 8.

The Twitter Search Bar

You can look at all the tweets on a particular subject by entering the keyword(s) in the Twitter search bar across the top of the screen. Topical subjects such as **climate change** or **Wimbledon**, for example, all yield large numbers of the very latest tweets.

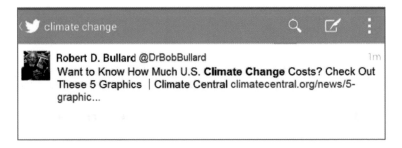

Hashtags

This is a hash symbol (**#**) you can place in front of an important keyword anywhere in a tweet, as in the **#floods** example below. If readers of the message tap over the hashtag, lots of tweets on the same subject are displayed.

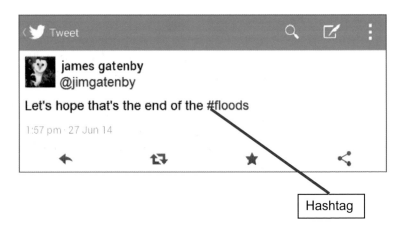

Some of the Main Features of Twitter

@

This is used to identify usernames in Twitter, e.g. **@johnbrown**. It also acts as a link to the user's Profile.

Activity

This shows what the people you're following have been doing and the tweets they have marked as *favorites*.

Direct Message (DM)

DM is a private message between two people who follow each other.

Discover

Helps you find people to follow, view top tweets and browse categories of tweets.

Favorite

If you like a tweet, tap the star underneath it to show you like it. Favorite tweets can be saved for viewing later.

Follow

Tap the **FOLLOW** button next to someone's name to start receiving their tweets on your Home page. You can follow anyone you choose and also **UNFOLLOW** them.

Hashtag

As discussed on the previous page, tapping the hashtag symbol displays all the other tweets which contain the same hashtag anywhere within them.

Mentions

When a **@username** appears *anywhere* in a tweet, this is known as a *mention*. This allows you to see all the tweets that include your **@username**.

Notifications

This allows you to view all your recent mentions, follows, retweets and interactions.

Profile

This page displays your biographical information and photos as show on page 77. It also shows the tweets you've posted.

Reply

A tweet posted in response to a tweet you've received. Tap the reply button on the tweet. The reply starts off with **@username**, unlike the original tweet.

Retweet (RT)

Forwarding to all of your followers a copy of a tweet you've received.

Timeline

The long list of tweets on your Home page from the people you follow. The latest tweets are at the top.

Trends

These are topics on Twitter which have been calculated by Twitter to be the most popular.

Tweet

A short message (140 characters or less) posted on the Internet to be viewed by your followers.

Getting Started With Twitter

Introduction

The procedure for getting up and running with Twitter is basically the same whatever type of tablet you are using. The main steps common to all platforms are as follows:

- Sign up with your e-mail address and decide on and enter a Twitter username and password.

- Twitter will present a list of your e-mail contacts already on Twitter so you can select those you wish to follow.

- A list of your contacts who are not yet on Twitter is displayed and you can invite them to join.

- Twitter suggests a list of people you may wish to follow, including friends and also celebrities who are tweeters.

- You can enter a personal Profile including a Profile photo and Header photo or image, if you wish.

- The Profile can also include a short description (up to 160 characters) of yourself or your company, etc.

Installing the Twitter App

If necessary, you can download the Twitter app from the appropriate app store, as shown below, in the same way as downloading the Facebook app, as described on page 28.

| iPad | Android | Windows |

Signing Up

All you need to create your own Twitter account is a computer connected to the Internet and a genuine e-mail address. When you tap the Twitter icon on your apps screen, the welcome page opens and you can either **Sign in** to an existing Twitter account or **Sign up** to create a new one, as shown below.

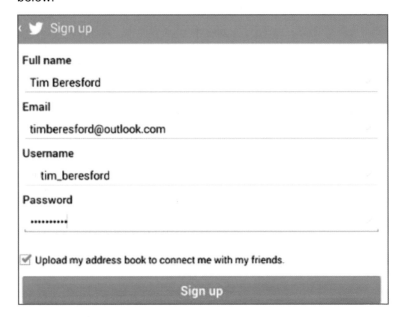

After entering your full name, e-mail address and password, Twitter assigns a **Username** to you, based on your e-mail address. If a name has already been used, Twitter suggests other usernames based on your own name or adds a character to your name as in **tim_beresford**, for example.

Following Friends and Contacts

From your e-mail contacts, Twitter presents a list of people who are already on Twitter, who you can choose to follow by tapping the icons shown on the right below to produce a tick, or by using **Select all**. Then their tweets will appear on your Home Timeline. Then tap the **Follow** button at the bottom right.

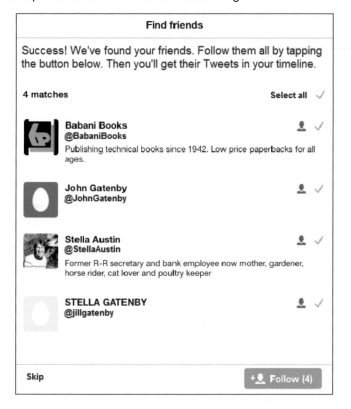

As shown above, the Profile photos, as opposed to the default egg-shaped icon, make it easier to identify someone you know on Twitter, as there may be a lot of people with the same name.

Inviting Friends to Join Twitter

Twitter also displays a list of your contacts who are not members of Twitter, as shown below.

Select the friends you wish to invite to join Twitter then tap the **Invite** button shown at the bottom right. If they accept, they will automatically become your followers.

Suggestions

Twitter produces lists of people, including celebrities, who you may choose to follow, as shown in the example below.

Tap the **Follow** button next to anyone whose tweets you want to appear on your Home page.

If you want to know more about a celebrity, etc., tap their name or Profile photo on the left of the screen. Their full size Profile photo, header photo and brief biography are displayed. Underneath the Profile, the messages they have tweeted or retweeted are displayed, as shown on the next page.

Unfollowing Someone

To stop following (or "unfollow") anyone, such as **antanddec** above, tap the **FOLLOWING** button shown on the right above. Next time you display the Profile the button will have changed to **FOLLOW**.

Creating Your Profile

During the sign up process you are given the chance to create your Profile. If you prefer, you can leave it blank and edit your Profile at any time after tapping your username or Profile photo.

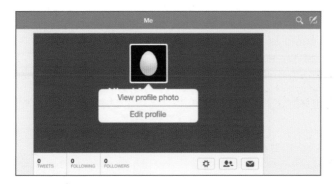

Tapping **Edit profile** in the window above opens the window shown below. Tapping **Photo** in the **Edit profile** window allows you to take a photo using your tablet's onboard camera to use as your Profile photo. Or you can browse the photos stored on your tablet to find a suitable photo. Tapping **Header** below lets you take a photo or browse for one to use as the Header, the wide photo across the top of the Profile.

Editing an Existing Profile

From your Home page tap the 3 dot menu button on the top right of the screen. Then tap your name or username as shown on the right. This opens your Profile as shown below. The small photo is your Profile photo, while the wide one is the Header.

The tweets or retweets that you've made are listed below your Profile, as shown on the previous page.

Tap your Profile photo followed by **Edit** or tap **Edit Profile** shown on the previous page to open the Profile window shown below.

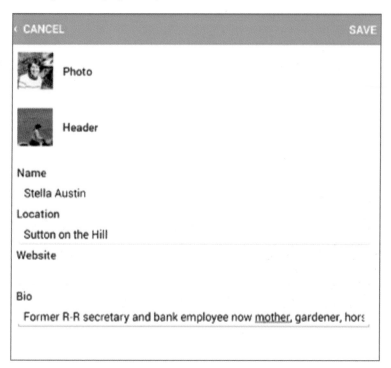

Tapping Photo or Header shown above allows you to insert different photos, as discussed on page 87. the **Name**, **Location** and **Website** can be edited or inserted after you tap in the appropriate slot. The **Bio** can be up to 160 characters long.

Finally tap **SAVE** shown in the top right-hand corner above.

A Tour of Twitter

Although the screen layouts are different, the basic functions and many of the icons are the same on Android, iPad and Windows tablets. For example, the Home page below on an iPad shows your Timeline and all the recent tweets you've sent and received from the people you're following. The main icons are down the left-hand side. Windows tablets have a similar layout.

Android tablets have a different **Home** screen, as shown below.

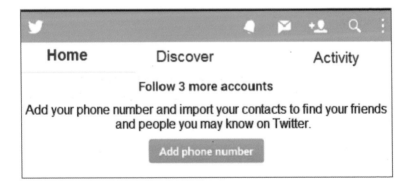

Listed below are some of the main Twitter features, which are common to the various platforms, unless stated otherwise.

Home

Displays your Home page or Timeline of all the tweets you've sent or received from the people you are following. Android uses the <u>Home</u> tab as shown near the bottom of the previous page.

Notifications

For example, informs you when new people are following you. Android uses the **Notifications** icon shown on the right.

Discover

Displays top tweets, who to follow, browse categories. Android uses the <u>Discover</u> tab shown at the bottom of the previous page.

Me

Displays your Profile and the tweets you've sent. On Android tap the 3 dot menu button and then your name.

Search

Enter names, usernames, keywords and hashtags to find people or organisations on Twitter.

New Tweet

Start a new tweet. Android uses a **What's happening?** bar which appears permanently at the bottom of the screen.

What's happening?

Messages (Android)

These are the private **Direct Messages** (**DM**s) between two people who follow each other. The icon appears on the Android toolbar as shown on the left.

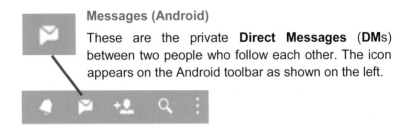

Messages (iPad)

The **Messages** icon on the iPad appears on the right of your Profile page. This is displayed after tapping the **Me** icon shown on the right and on the previous   page.

Find people (Android)

The **Find people** icon on Android suggests a list of people for you to follow. There is also a list of categories of people, such as television, government, music and fashion.

   Connect (Windows)

Windows tablets have the **Home**, **Discover** and **Me** icons as described on the previous page. They also use the **Connect** tab shown above to display who has followed you, retweeted or favorited your tweets and to show all your **@replies** and **@mentions**. The **Connec**t tab has been replaced by **Notifications** shown on page 91 on Android and iPad tablets.

Signing Out of Twitter

Twitter remembers your username and password every time you start a session. If you want to sign in with a different Twitter username and password, or let someone else use your tablet, there is no obvious button for signing out. However, as described below, you can sign out of Twitter by deleting your Twitter account on your tablet. This doesn't remove your username and password from the Twitter social network.

Signing Out of Twitter on an Android Tablet

From the 3 dot menu button shown on the right, select
Settings, as shown below.

Then tap your username, followed by **Sign out** at the bottom of the next screen. After tapping **OK** to **remove all Twitter data from this device**, you are presented with a welcome screen allowing you to sign up or sign in with a different username and password.

You can still sign in to Twitter on this or any other tablet, using the original username and password for the deleted account.

Sign up a different account	Sign In

Signing Out of Twitter on an iPad

Tap the **Settings** icon on the main iPad apps screen.

Then, if necessary, scroll up and tap **Twitter** in the left-hand panel of the **Settings** screen. Then tap your **@username** in the right-hand panel, as shown below.

Next tap **Delete Account** as shown below.

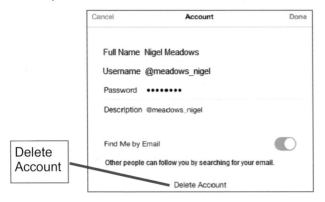

Delete Account

Click **Delete** again to remove the account from the tablet. As before you can sign in with another username and password or with the username and password you've just deleted.

Signing Out of Twitter on a Windows Tablet

Swipe in from the top of the screen and then tap the icon shown on the right, on the menu bar across the top of the screen. Then tap the cross shown below, against your name on the left of the screen, to sign out of Twitter.

Posting and Receiving Tweets

Introduction

When you first start using Twitter, you'll not have any followers and won't have posted any tweets. Twitter will quickly suggest lots of people for you to follow, as discussed earlier. In fact you could use Twitter without any followers and without posting any tweets. Simply use Twitter to follow celebrities, such as Jeremy Clarkson, with nearly four million followers, as shown below.

However, if you want to post tweets of your own, you need to get some followers – otherwise nobody will ever see your pearls of wisdom. You can use Twitter to have a dialogue with friends or family if you are all signed up to Twitter and following each other.

Finding Someone and Following Them

Enter their name in the Twitter search bar. Obviously a Profile photo helps to identify the correct person in a long list.

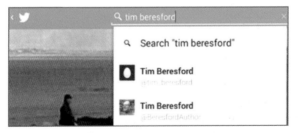

After tapping the person's name, their Profile page appears, allowing you to tap the **Follow** button shown on the right. Then the button changes to **Following**, also shown on the right.

Posting a Tweet

Stella taps **What's happening?** at the bottom of her Profile page on her Android tablet and enters the text (up to 140 characters) into the new tweet window, as shown below. (On an iPad or Windows tablet tap the New Tweet icon shown on the right).

The icon on the bottom left above allows Twitter to include your current location in the tweet. The small icon on the right above allows you to include a photo in the tweet. This can be taken using a camera built into the tablet or by selecting a photo from the Internal Storage of the tablet, as shown on the right. Photos are discussed in more detail in Chapter 10. After tapping the blue **Tweet** button, shown in the New

Tweet window above, a copy of Stella's tweet appears on her own Profile page, as shown below. The blue text beginning pic.twitter.com/ is a link to open the photo of the cat.

StellaAustin @StellaAustin9
Our cat Meddy has evicted some pigeons from their nest, six feet up in one of our trees. She now sleeps in it.
pic.twitter.com/mKdLqbRFOS

Responding to Tweets

Once you follow people on Twitter, their tweets will appear on the Timeline on your Home page, along with the tweets you've posted. After reading a tweet, there are many ways you can respond to it.

- Post a *reply*.
- *Retweet* it to all of your followers.
- Mark it as a *favorite* for viewing later and to tell the original tweeter that you liked their tweet.
- Click on a *hashtag* (e.g. *#climate*) within a tweet to find other tweets on the same topic as the hashtag.

After Stella taps **Tweet**, as discussed on the previous page, the tweet will be very quickly available to be viewed by any of Stella's followers. For example, Tim, a follower of Stella, receives a copy of Stella's tweet on his Home page on his iPad, as shown below.

Depending on a tablet's Settings, the image may not appear, just a blue text link starting **pic.twitter.com/**, as shown at the bottom of page 96. Tap the tweet to display a large version complete with the image, as shown on the next page.

At the top of the tweet are the full name and username of the person who posted the tweet. The icons at the bottom right above have the following functions.

 Reply to the person who posted the tweet. The reply is delivered to your followers and those of the originator.

 Retweet, i.e. forward a tweet you've received on to all of your   followers.

 Mark a tweet to show you liked it and keep the tweet for viewing later in the **Favorites** section of your Profile.

Replying to a Tweet

One of Stella's followers, Tim, taps the **Reply** icon to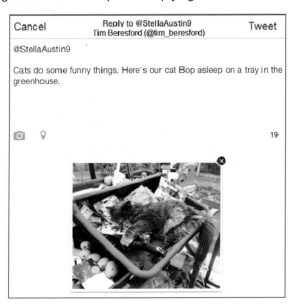
open the window shown below on Tim's iPad. Twitter
automatically inserts Stella's name as the sender of the original
message and Tim as the person replying.

Cancel	Reply to @StellaAustin9 Tim Beresford (@tim_beresford)	Tweet

@StellaAustin9

Cats do some funny things. Here's our cat Bop asleep on a tray in the
greenhouse.

Like the Android Twitter app, the iPad app has icons
to include your current location and insert a photo in
a tweet or reply. The photo can be
taken with the tablet's camera or
selected from the Internal Storage.

In the above example, the image of
the cat was transferred to my iPad
from my PC, using DropBox, discussed in Chapter 10. Then the
image was saved in **Photos/Camera Roll** on the iPad. The
photo is then available for inserting in the tweet using the
Choose existing photo option shown above.

Receiving a Reply

Stella receives Tim's reply to her tweet on her Home page on her Android tablet as shown below.

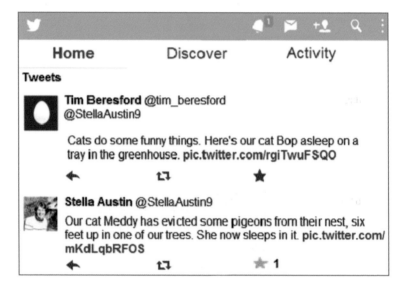

The extract from Stella's Home page above shows her original tweet at the bottom with the reply from her follower Tim above it. The original tweet shows the tweeter's name, while the reply shows both the respondent's name and the originator's name below it.

Favorites

In the example above, the **Favorite** star icon has changed to gold with a **1** against it, indicating that one person (Tim) has made the tweet one of their **Favorites**. This provides positive feedback to Stella about her tweet and will allow Tim to retrieve the tweet quickly if he wants to look at it in the future. This is done after tapping **Favorites** on his Profile page.

Viewing Images in Tweets

In the screenshot on the previous page, the images posted with the tweets are not shown, only the blue text links beginning **pic.twitter.com/**. To view the full image tap the blue text link.

Android and iPad

To switch on the preview of images in tweets on your Home page, on an Android tap the 3 dot menu button on your Profile page, shown on the right, then select **Settings** and **General** and make sure **Image previews** is ticked.

On the iPad, tap **Me**, tap the gear wheel icon shown on the left of the three shown on the right, then tap **Settings** and switch on **Image previews**.

Retweeting

If you think a tweet you receive will be of interest to your followers, tap the **Retweet** icon shown on the right. As shown on page 98, this appears on the bottom of the tweets from the people you are following. The retweeted tweet will then appear on the Home page of all your followers.

The **Retweet** icon at the bottom of the tweet displayed on the originator's tablet is highlighted and includes a **1** to show the tweet has been retweeted, as shown below.

Using RT@username

Instead of using the **Retweet** button you can use the New Tweet window to forward a message to your followers. Type in **RT@username** to give credit to the original tweeter. Then copy the original message. You can modify the original tweet and add text of your own, up to 140 characters for the whole tweet.

| Home | Discover | Activity |

Tim Beresford @tim_beresford
RT@StellaAustin9 Cats do some funny things. Here's our cat Bop asleep on a tray in the greenhouse.

Deleting Tweets

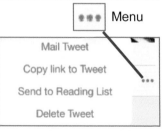

Menu

You can't delete tweets that other people have posted. To delete one of your own tweets, tap on the tweet in your Home page. On an iPad tap the three dot menu button and select **Delete Tweet** as shown on the right above. On an Android or Windows tablet tap the dustbin icon shown on the right.

Hashtags

You often see within the text of a tweet, something like **#tourdefrance**. The hash sign (**#**) followed by a keyword such as **tourdefrance**, for example, is called a *hashtag*. The hashtag makes it very easy for you to find all the Tweets on popular topics by entering the hashtag into the Twitter search bar. You can create your own hashtags in the tweets you post. The hashtag search produces a list of the latest tweets which are specifically about the word or words in the hashtag. For example, typing **#tourdefrance** into the Twitter search bar produces the following small sample.

Trends

These are tweets which Twitter calculates are currently increasing rapidly in popularity. **Trending** appears in the **Discover** feature on Android, iPad and Windows tablets. Hashtags which are very popular often become trending topics. Trends may be based on your location or worldwide.

Key Facts: Posting and Receiving Tweets

- A new tweet can be up to 140 characters long and after posting appears on your Timeline and on the Timelines of the people following you.

- The full name and **@username** of the sender appear at the top of a tweet. Tapping either opens their **Profile**.

- An icon enabling you to send a **Reply** appears on the tweets you receive. Replies start off with the **@username** of the person posting the original Tweet.

- The **Retweet** button allows you to forward to your followers a tweet received from someone else.

- You can also enter **RT@username** and type the text of the original message and any text of your own, to give credit to the original Tweeter.

- A **Hashtag** such as **#windfarms** in a tweet is a link making it easy to find other tweets on the same subject.

- Your **Mentions** are tweets that have your username anywhere within them, so this includes replies to you.

- **Trends** are links to topics calculated by Twitter to be currently most popular, worldwide or more locally.

- You can post a photo in a tweet. A recipient may need to tap a blue text link to open the photograph.

- A Tweet can include a link to a Web page, typed or pasted in. The Web site is opened by tapping the link.

- A link in a Tweet can give your current **Location**. Tapping the link opens a map, photos and information.

- A **Direct message** is sent to just one of your followers.

- **Favorites** saves the Tweets you want to keep and tells the original Tweeter that you liked their Tweet.

- You can't **Edit** your Tweets but you can **Delete** them from your Timeline and from your followers' Timelines.

Putting Photos Onto Your Tablet

Introduction

Photos and videos play a major role in social networks like Facebook and Twitter. With families and friends scattered around the world, the posting of your latest news and photos is an excellent way to keep in touch. This is particularly valuable if you're not able to travel for any reason. Perhaps there are relatives you've never seen or a brother or sister on the other side of the world you've lost contact with.

There are several ways you can put photos and videos onto the Internal Storage of a tablet. The photos and videos are then readily available for viewing on your tablet at any time and can be included in the updates you post with Facebook and the tweets you post with Twitter, as discussed earlier in this book.

Some of the main methods are:

- Taking a photo or making a video with one of the tablet's own built-in cameras.

- Copying photos onto the tablet from a standalone digital camera or a camera's SD or Micro SD card.

- Copying photos saved on a flash drive or memory stick.

- Copying photos that have been stored on a laptop or desktop computer. The source might include old photo prints on paper which you've scanned and saved.

- Sharing and saving photos that have been sent to you using Facebook or Twitter or by e-mail.

Using a Tablet's Built-in Cameras

Tablets generally have two cameras:

- A relatively low resolution camera (e.g. 2MP) on the front of the tablet for use in video calls using apps such as Skype and FaceTime and for taking 'selfies'.

- A higher resolution camera (e.g. 5MP) on the back of the camera for taking general photographs and making videos.

Tap the camera icon on your App screen. It will probably launch the rear camera ready for you to take an ordinary photo. If you want to make a video call, when using Skype for example, the front camera launches automatically showing your face, etc. This front camera can also be used to take a 'selfie' for inclusion in a Facebook update or a tweet on Twitter.

Android Tablets

Switching Between Front and Rear Cameras

Tap the **Camera** app shown above then tap the small 3 button menu icon shown on the right. Then tap the lower icon shown on the right and below to switch between front and rear cameras.

Selecting Photo or Video Mode

Swipe in from the left and tap either **Camera** or **Video** from the menu on the left of the screen, shown here on the right.

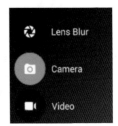

Taking a Photo Android Tablets

Select **Camera** as shown on the previous page at the bottom right. Then tap the black and white Camera icon, shown here on the right, to take a photo with the selected camera. You will hear a noise as the photo is taken.

Making a Video

Select **Video** as shown on the previous page at the bottom right. Then tap the video camera icon shown on the right to start recording. Tap the square icon shown on the right to end the recording.

Viewing Photos and Videos

Photos and videos can now be viewed, as shown below, after tapping the **Gallery** icon, shown on the right, and then selecting the **Camera** Album, shown below.

Tap on a photo, then tap the 3 button menu icon shown on the right. Then tap the sharing icon shown on the lower right to display a drop-down menu. Selecting **Facebook** or **Twitter** from this menu opens a window for a new post or tweet, with the photo already inserted.

Using the Built-in Cameras on an iPad

The methods for taking photos and videos on an iPad are basically the same as those described for Android tablets on the previous two pages, the main differences being the icons, shown below. Apart from the Camera App icon shown at the top below, these all appear down the right-hand side of the Camera screen.

   Start the Camera App

   Switch between front and rear cameras

   Swipe up or down to select **Photo** or **Video**

   Take a single photograph

   Video selected after swiping down

Start recording video

Stop recording video

Viewing Photos and Videos on an iPad

To view the new photos and videos you've taken using the built-in cameras on the iPad, tap the icon for the **Photos** app shown on the right. The photos and videos are displayed in the **Camera Roll** as shown below.

As shown above, you can select certain photos, add them to albums or share them on YouTube, Facebook or e-mail, etc.

More on the Camera Roll — Android and iPad

The Camera Roll is like the film in the traditional camera — it stores all the photos and videos you take with the built-in cameras on the tablet. When you tap the camera icon in an update or tweet, the **Camera Roll** is displayed, as shown below. Then select the photo(s) to include in your update or tweet.

Importing Photos to a Tablet
Android Tablets

Many tablets don't have the full size USB port needed to connect a camera or other devices. However, the *Micro USB* port built into many tablets can easily be converted to a full-size USB port using an OTG (On The Go) cable, as shown below.

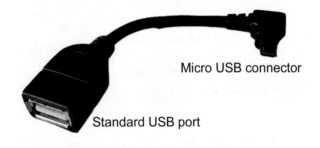

Micro USB connector

Standard USB port

An OTG cable

The OTG cable can be used for connecting the following USB devices to a tablet, for the copying of photos and other files.

- Digital camera.
- USB card reader.
- USB flash drive/ memory stick.

Connecting a Digital Camera

Digital cameras are normally provided with a cable which has a USB connector or plug. This is used for charging the camera's battery and can also be used for copying photos to a tablet. Insert the OTG cable into the Micro USB port on the tablet. Insert the USB connector on the camera cable into the USB port on the OTG cable. Then connect the other end of the cable to the camera. The tablet should detect the camera and you then import the photos, as discussed shortly.

Connecting an SD Card Using a Card Reader

It may be more convenient to import photos from an SD card which has been removed from a camera. USB card readers are available, as shown on the right, which plug directly into the USB port on the OTG cable shown on the previous page. Some card readers have a range of slots of different sizes to accommodate different types of SD card.

USB card reader with SD card inserted

Connecting a Micro SD Card

Some tablets, such as the Tesco Hudl and the Samsung Galaxy range, have a slot for a Micro SD card. This can be used to provide additional storage on the tablet but also as a camera card. An adapter the size of a standard SD card enables the Micro SD card to be used in a standard digital camera.

Micro SD adapter and card

Then the Micro SD card, complete with new photos, can be removed from the adapter and inserted into the slot in the tablet. The photo files can then be imported, as discussed shortly.

Connecting a USB Flash Drive

Photos stored on a *USB flash drive* (or *memory stick*) can be imported into a tablet after inserting the flash drive into the USB port on an OTG cable, shown on the previous page.

USB flash drive

USB connector or plug

Transferring the Photos

Having connected a camera card to the tablet in one of the ways discussed on the previous two pages, they now need to be copied or transferred to the Internal Storage of the tablet. Your tablet may not have the necessary file manager app to import the files, but several are available for downloading free from the Play Store, as discussed in Chapter 3. These include the Nexus Media Importer, which works with Android tablets in general.

The **Copy** icon shown on the right and above, saves the selected photos in the **Pictures** folder in the Internal Storage of the tablet.

Tapping the **Share** icon shown on the right and above allows you to send copies of the photo to numerous destinations such as Facebook and Twitter.

Accessing Photos on a Micro SD Card

This is very simple with tablets having a Micro SD card slot. Fully insert the card. Tap the **Gallery** icon shown on the right. The new photos show up as a new **Album** in the Gallery. Here they can be shared to your Facebook or Twitter accounts, etc., after tapping the **Share** icon shown on the right. If you leave the Micro SD card in the   slot in the tablet, the photos will be accessible in the Camera Roll for inserting in updates and tweets in Facebook and Twitter.

Importing Photos to an iPad

The port on an iPad used to connect the battery charging cable can accommodate an adapter which houses a camera's SD card. There are also adapters which provide a full-size USB socket, allowing devices such as USB card readers and flash drives to be connected to an iPad, as discussed earlier. Earlier iPads use the large 30-pin adapter shown on the left below. Also shown is the later 8-pin Lightning adapter. Adapters are also available to convert 30-pin connectors to the 8-pin standard.

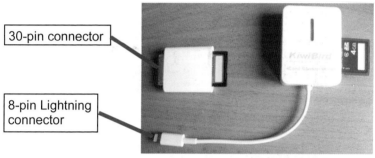

30-pin connector

8-pin Lightning connector

iPad SD card readers

After you connect the card reader and SD card to the iPad, the **Import** icon pops up at the bottom of the screen, as shown on the right. Tap the **Import** icon and all the photos on the card are quickly displayed. Then

Import

tap **Import All** to copy the photos to the iPad, where they can be accessed on the Camera Roll by Facebook and Twitter.

Importing Photos to a Windows Tablet

Using the Built-in Cameras

From the Windows 8.1 Start screen tap the **Camera** tile shown on the right.

Select single photo or video by tapping the appropriate icon on the right of the screen, as shown on the right.

Switching Between Front and Rear Cameras

Swipe up from the bottom of the screen and tap **Change camera** shown on the right. The front camera is used in video calls or for taking 'selfies'. The rear camera takes photos and videos like a standalone digital camera. Tap the camera icon to take a photo or tap the video icon to start and stop a video recording.

Connecting a Camera, Card Reader or Flash Drive

Larger Windows tablets like the Surface and Surface Pro have a full size USB port, making it easy to connect devices such as cameras and card readers, as discussed earlier. Smaller Windows tablets use a Micro USB port, which can be converted to full USB using an OTG cable, as shown on page 110.

Transferring the Photos

The operating system used on Windows tablets is the same or very similar to that used on most desktop and laptop computers. So the Windows tablet has the File Explorer (formerly known as Windows Explorer) for managing files such as photos.

When you connect a camera, card reader or flash drive to a Windows tablet, the device is detected and appears as **Removable Disk (E:)** in the Windows File Explorer as shown on the right and at the top of the next page. Several USB

devices can be connected to a tablet simultaneously, using a multi-port *USB hub*.

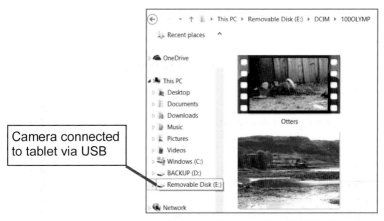

Camera connected to tablet via USB

Photos displayed in File Explorer

As shown above in the File Explorer, the video and photo are in a folder called **100OLYMP**, within a folder **DCIM** on the camera which has been designated **Removable Disk (E:)**.

▶ This PC ▶ Removable Disk (E:) ▶ DCIM ▶ 100OLYMP

The File Explorer makes it easy to copy photos from the camera or card reader to a folder on the Windows tablet (and vice versa). Simply drag and drop the photo over the new folder or use **Copy** and **Paste**. (Hold over a photo to display the menu).

To insert a photo in a Facebook update or a tweet on Twitter, you can browse all the photos on the Windows tablet and choose those you wish to upload.

Managing Android and iPad Files Using a PC

You can use the File Explorer (or Windows Explorer) on a laptop or desktop Windows PC to manage files on an Android or iPad. Connect the Android or iPad to a USB port on the PC using the tablet's charging cable. The Android or iPad appears in the File Explorer as just another device, as shown on the next page.

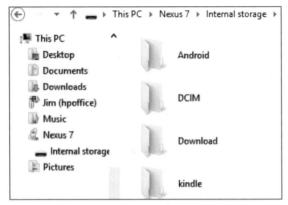

The Internal Storage of an Android
tablet (Nexus 7) viewed on a PC

The PC File Explorer can be used to manage the files and folders on the tablet, i.e. **Copy**, **Paste**, **Delete**, **Rename**, etc.

Cloud Computing

This is a good way to copy files such as photos between all your computers — tablet, desktop or laptop, etc. The Clouds, such as Google Drive, iCloud and SkyDrive, etc., are actually Internet storage computers. My own favourite is Dropbox (**www.dropbox.com**). The basic features of Dropbox are as follows:

- Download Dropbox to every computer you use — Android, iPad and Windows tablets, laptop, desktop PCs.

- Create a Dropbox username and password.

- Save your latest photos and other files in the Dropbox folder on any one of your computers.

- Sign into Dropbox on any computer. Your latest photos are automatically *synced* (copied) to all your computers.

- Photos can be copied from Dropbox on a tablet to other locations, e.g. the Photos library or an album on a tablet.

Index

3G or 4G 11, 18, 20

A

Airplane mode 17
Android 4, 6
  apps 22
  installing 28
  standard OS 6
  tweaked OS 7

C

Camera, connecting 110
Camera Roll 109
Cloud computing 116

F

Facebook 1, 23
  account, confirming 33
  app, installing 28
  audience selectors ....
  .... 24, 32, 34, 41, 57, 63
  Browse 51
  Chatting 71
  Comment 65
  Contacts 50
  Cover photo 34, 46
  e-mail address 25, 26
  features 35
  Friend Lists 55-58
  Friends 3, 24, 25, 47, 52
  Launching Facebook 34
  Like 65
  Messages 69
  News Feed 60
  Poke 72

Facebook (continued)
  Privacy 25, 32, 41
  Profile 24, 34, 37
    editing 40
    Picture 31, 34, 42-45
  Search 49
  security, privacy 25, 32
  Settings menu 68
  Share 65
  signing in 59
  signing up 29
  Status Update 62, 63
    inserting web link 66
    posting 64
  Timeline 10, 24, 34, 61
    posting on friend's 67
  using Facebook 59
Flight mode 17, 20

I

Importing photos 110-114
Internet access point 12
Internet, connecting 11
iOS 4, 5

M

Managing files on a tablet
  using a PC 115
Micro SD card 111
Micro USB port 110
Mobile broadband
  dongle 18
  hotspot 18

O

Operating system 4
OTG cable........................ 110

P

Password, router 15
Phablet............................. 3
Profile information 32

R

Router, password 15

S

SD card 111
SIM card slot on a tablet 18
Smartphone 3
Social Networking 1, 2, 3
Stylus 5
Switching cameras.................
.... 106, 108, 114

T

Tablet..................................... 3
Tethering........................ 11, 19
Tweet 73, 80
Twitter 2, 73
   @ 79
   140 character limit......... 74
   Activity............................ 79
   app.................................. 81
   deleting tweets 102
   Direct Message (DM).... 79
   Discover........................ 79
   Favorite.................. 79, 100
   finding someone............ 95
   Following............ 79, 83-86
   Hashtags......... 78, 79, 103
   inviting friends............... 84

Twitter (continued)
   Mentions........................80
   Messages 75
   Notifications 80
   Photos 76, 105
   posting a tweet 96
   Profile 80
      creating....................87
      editing......................88
      information...............77
   receiving a reply 100
   Reply 80, 99
   responding to tweets 97
   Retweet (RT) 80, 102
   RT@username 102
   search bar 78
   signing out.....................93
   signing up 82
   Suggestions...................85
   Timeline.........................80
   tour 90
   Trends 80, 103
   unfollowing someone.....86
   viewing images 101

U

USB flash drive................111
USB port...........................110
Using cameras..........106 -114

W

Web browser 21
Wi-Fi 12-17
Windows 8.1, RT 8.1 ...4, 8, 9